THE OFFICIAL
BADGE
COLLECTOR'S GUIDE
FROM THE 1890s TO THE 1980s

Frank R Setchfield

About the author

Frank Setchfield is a primary school teacher who lives in Loughborough, Leicestershire. He started collecting badges twenty years ago and now has over 20,000. He runs the Badge Collector's Circle.

Longman Group UK Limited,
Longman House, Burnt Mill, Harlow,
Essex CM20 2JE, England
and Associated Companies throughout the world.

© Longman Group UK Limited 1986
All rights reserved; no part of this publication
may be reproduced, stored in a retrieval system,
or transmitted in any form or by any means, electronic,
mechanical, photocopying, recording, or otherwise,
without the prior written permission of the Publishers.

First published 1986

British Library Cataloguing in Publication Data

The official Badge Collector's Guide from the 1890s to the 1980s
1. Badges
737'.24   TS761
ISBN 0-582-89306-2

Set in 10/12 and 9/10 'Monophoto' Plantin Light
Printed in Spain
by TONSA, San Sebastian.

Acknowledgements

The author would like to extend special thanks to Thomas Fattorini of Thomas Fattorini Ltd. Thanks are also due to these badge manufacturers: B Sanders and Sons; London Emblem Company; Universal Button Company; R E V Gomm; W O Lewis (Badges) Ltd; Kildsware (formerly Jemah).

Thanks to all the members of the Badge Collectors Circle whose work is published in a bi-monthly newsletter. Thanks are also due to all the museums, groups, organizations and companies who have supplied information about their badges.

Special thanks are owed to my mother Mary Setchfield for her efforts on the typewriter.

Contents

For she who has suffered!—Rosemary—
and for those who didn't badger me,
Jethro, Joshua and Florence.

Introduction

A COLLECTION OF BADGES gives a unique insight into the past. A badge can tell you who the wearer voted for, what they did in their spare time, or had for breakfast. This book, the first to cover the whole spectrum of lapel badges, sets out to reveal just some of these fascinating, sometimes forgotten, details. Most of the badges discussed here are 'button' badges, but enamel, metal, plastic, card and even leatherette badges are also included.

Such a task is mammoth: like the iceberg theory, for every lapel badge shown here there are many more different ones. But while this book can only touch the tip of the subject, I hope to give a hint of what the whole iceberg is like.

Outside the scope of this book are badges worn on uniforms such as military or police badges, those sewn on (sometimes called patches), those stuck on (stickers) and paper flags. Paper flags, once common, now almost extinct, have been replaced mainly by stickers, and although both are directly related to lapel badges they are not included in here.

Moreover, all the badges date from the latter part of the nineteenth century, and the majority since 1945. Before the Second World War the majority of badges were metal or enamel. Since 1945 the button badge has come into its own, particularly in the badge 'boom' periods of the 1960s and 1970s, a development directly related to the youth culture. Plastic badges, too, have emerged since the 1950s as the plastics industry developed.

Types of badges

A distinction should be made at the outset between metal and enamelled badges, and button or plastic badges. Metal and enamelled badges are items of considerable quality, and as many of these were made before 1939, they are often prized by collectors. As a reflection of their quality, they are sometimes known as brooches. Button badges however, are not just a poor substitute, even if they are much cheaper. They can be colourful, eyecatching, and beautifully finished. A button badge can also be made very quickly whereas metal and enamel badges take much longer. Thus designs for button badges are more immediate, often reacting quickly to events with slogans such as 'All troops out of the Falklands now' or 'The King is Dead' (Elvis Presley).

From 1977 to 1985 roughly 1,000 million button badges were made for British consumption. Even this conservative estimate means that two and a half badges have been made for each person in Britain every year since 1977. Of these 1,000 million badges there at least 100,000 different designs. The throwaway nature of button badges means that many of these sink without trace. But many badges arouse a greater interest and are now avidly collected, particularly by children.

Metal and enamelled badges have always been collectable, and those for trade unions, Butlins, Robertson's, gollies and football clubs are among the most popular. Many are very ornate and reflect a craftsmanship developed in Victorian times. Since the 1970s imita-

tion or 'pretend enamels' have crept into the market to satisfy the demand for cheaper badges. These often consist of printed plastic stuck onto a metal base. Thousands are manufactured in the Far East, as well as in Britain.

The badges in this book have been grouped by topic, but any categorization comes down to personal choice in the end. There are simply so many overlaps that a perfect catalogue would be impossible without cross-referencing. For example, 'Anglia Television 1977 Jubilee Year' could be placed under television, royalty or commemorative. Similarly, 'Young Ornithologists Club Save the Birds' designs could be placed under children's clubs or environmental. The index may help you to find a particular badge.

Collectors can gain further information by joining clubs such as the Badge Collectors Circle. Details are given in the section on collecting at the end of the book.

In this journey through time with badges I have tried to maintain a balance and describe as many as possible within the space allowed. Inevitably there will be more reference to button badges than anything else as far more have been produced, especially since the 1960s. But the quantity of badges is such that each page of this book could easily become a book itself.

Button Badges

History and development

A button badge consists of: a shell (or cup) usually of tin (but sometimes aluminium); a ring and pin fixture or a solid back and pin fixture; and a print, which is either bonded to acetate or simply covered
with acetate without being bonded.

The term 'button badge' is not a common one yet in Britain, most
people preferring 'lapel badge' or 'tin badge'. 'Button badge' is, however, more accurate as the very first ones were made on button-making machinery, and were referred to as pinback buttons.

The techniques of bending metal and wrapping cloth round were
well established in the latter half of the nineteenth century by button
manufacturers. The invention of celluloid in the 1870s gave rise to
new possibilities, and as early as 1888 celluloid was being used for
bookmarks and advertising cards.

The first button badges

Button badges, something like we know them today, were first patented in America by the Whitehead and Hoag Company of Newark, New
Jersey. A paper print was covered by a thin layer of celluloid wrapped
around a metal disc, with a stick pin in the back. Three patents appear
on early Whitehead and Hoag button badges – for 3 December 1893,
6 December 1895 and 23 March 1896. The 1893 patent was for a
clothing button covered wholly in cloth, and Whitehead and Hoag
purchased rights to this patent from another company in order to protect their other claims. The 1895 patent concerned the rear of the
badge and the stick-pin fixing, and was filed by George Adams, as-
signor to Whitehead and Hoag. The 1896 patent completed their
series, and the claim reads:

> In a badge pin or button, in combination with a shell having a
> marginal rim or bead, a covering bearing an inscription, design,
> emblem or the like, over said shell and having its edge turned
> down over said marginal rim, a ring or collet in said shell placed
> over the edge of said covering to hold or secure the latter in posi-
> tion, and a bar or pin having one of its ends bent to form a holding
> position adapted to be secured in said ring or collet, substantially
> as and for the purposes set forth.

These first button badges were issued in 1896 in America, where
whole sets were given away with cigarettes instead of cards, or with
candy or chewing gum. The McKinley and Bryon presidential campaign of 1896 also stimulated the novelty. Whitehead and Hoag soon
set up agents in London and badges were exported to Britain for
Queen Victoria's Diamond Jubilee of 1897. Further imports followed, featuring Boer War generals and, in 1902, Edward VII Coronation designs.

By 1902 British button manufacturers had begun to produce button
badges, and a series showing Boer War generals are amongst the first
produced in Britain. The quality of these is inferior to the American
imports, and no maker's name is carried, but it is believed that a few

button manufacturers were experimenting with the process. John Nicholls, the retired managing director of B Sanders and Sons of Bromsgrove, recalls his father telling him that his grandfather had done just so, but a fire at the factory in 1958 destroyed these early samples.

Early British button badges

By 1905 American imports had mostly stopped and British manufacturers had begun to produce button badges in earnest. However, the sort of quantities produced in the United States were never matched in Britain until the button badge booms of the 1960s and 1970s. Only badges for royal occasions, and schools and officers badges really sold in big numbers.

In the early years of George V (1911–14) there was a fashion craze for buttons and button badges (at this time there was little distinction) portraying actresses and other personalities, although no lady of breeding would associate with a man who wore one. As late as the 1930s these badges were still referred to as 'celluloid buttons'. Even in the 1936 Universal Button Company catalogue they are referred to as celluloid buttons on one page, and on another as celluloid badges. Four different fittings were on offer: the stick pin, stud fitting, wire brooch fitting, and the best brooch fitting. The 'wire brooch' was what we would now call standard, and the 'best brooch' was a solid back with a brooch-pin arrangement. The locking-tongue standard wire-brooch fitting had been patented on 30 May 1899 by the Advertising Novelty Company of Newark, New Jersey, but did not become common until much later. The Universal Button Company also produced oval button badges, but these, like all pre-war examples, are rare.

Apart from the Universal Button Company, other prewar British manufacturers included Thomas Fattorini Ltd, The Merchants Portrait Company (London) and White and Lambert (believed to have begun in 1908).

Tin badges

Button badges printed directly on to tin using a lithographic technique, similar to the way in which a beer can may be printed, began in 1916. One big advantage was that a ring was not required, as there was no print or acetate to grip. Moreover, these badges worked out cheaper for mass orders, although smaller runs were not usually undertaken. Despite these advantages, however, lithographs have never really rivalled the traditional acetate badges, chiefly because of their liability to scratching and tinny appearance. However, they were still made after 1945 and Anterior was one, if not the only, producer in Britain. Since the 1970s the process has been commonplace in the Far East and many such badges are actually imported, especially from Hong Kong.

Button badge manufacture

Today there is only a handful of major button-badge manufacturers in Britain, although judging by the variety of names on the folds of button badges there may appear to be many more. In fact, while that

'Children are by nature Badge wearers', asserts the 1939 catalogue for Thomas Fattorini Ltd, an early British badge manufacturer. Illustrated is a typical prewar range: badges advertising bread, dog food and cigarettes, alongside those for more charitable purposes—together with the perennial exhortation to 'Buy British'.

CELLULOID BADGES

Children are by nature Badge wearers and will carry your message for you everywhere. A few thousand of these inexpensive Celluloid Badges distributed to children will more than repay the outlay.

They will still be in use when other forms of Advertising are worn out.

We will send a special design post free on request.

May we send you a quotation, without obligation.

Badges are an unqualified success as money raisers at Carnivals, Pageants, etc. They cost so little, can be made most attractive and are readily sold at a handsome profit. Secretaries have told us how helpful these Badges have been and repeat orders confirm their success.

THOMAS FATTORINI LTD. REGENT STREET WORKS **BIRMINGHAM, 1**

PLEASE NOTE THE **THOMAS** IN OUR NAME AS SIMILAR FIRMS ARE **NOT** THE SAME

CHILDREN'S CORNER CELLULOID

name may refer to the manufacturer, more usually it will be the name of the publisher, printer or indeed just the agent, since the major manufacturers do not work directly. Agents also may wish it to appear that the badge has come straight from them. And more often than not there will be no name at all on the back of a design.

In 1985 the major button badge companies were the Universal Button Company, Better Badges and the London Emblem Company in the London area, and W O Lewis (formerly White and Lambert), Baynham and Stanfield, The Button Badge Company and B Sanders and Sons of Bromsgrove in the West Midlands area.

One of the largest British manufacturers estimated that from June 1984 to June 1985 it produced approximately 28 million badges, in lots ranging from 1,000 or 2,000 to major runs of 50,000 or 100,000. This means at least 2,000 different designs.

The manufacturing process

The major manufacturers are involved in all levels of production, from the artwork to the printing, laminating and pressing. However, some of the major manufacturers send badges out to be made up by others, or they buy in the backs and shells. Many of the names on the side of a badge refer to those responsible for the artwork and printing. Before being made up the prints may be bonded to the acetate, or a separate piece of melonex acetate cut to size. The laminated or bonded badges usually have a better finish.

Apart from print-room staff and those who make up the badges, people are employed to make the shells (or cups), rings, backs and pins. B Sanders and Sons of Bromsgrove, like most of the main manufacturers, obtain their pins from Whitecroft and Scovill of Lydney. (Older button badges often employed brass for their pins.) B Sanders and Sons is one of the few companies who make their own shells and backs. For this reason a toolmaker is an essential part of their staff, the presses not always running smoothly. In 1985 they made round shells in the following diameters: 1 in (25 mm), 1¼ in (32 mm), 1½ in (38 mm), 1¾ in (45 mm), 2⅛ in (55 mm) and 3 in (77 mm), together with an oblong and square shape.

Since very few manufacturers are involved in the complete process, the button badge on your lapel is often the product of a combination of companies. Furthermore, some designs are made up by more than one manufacturer which explains why the same design can sometimes be found with a completely different pin fitting or ring. Similarly some designs, such as the 'Tufty Club', may be reordered every few years resulting in slight variations.

Design modifications

After 1945 the stick pin feature all but disappeared, except on the tiny ¾ in (19 mm) badges where a wire brooch fixture, with locking tongue, was not possible. Solid backs became a little commoner on larger badges in the 1960s, but little else changed until the early 1970s.

Crimps

White and Lambert are the only firm who 'crimp' the design onto the shell of the badge rather than secure it with a ring. Apart from the staff cutting their fingers on the sharp edges of the rings, putting a

Types of button badge backs

Button badges are surprisingly varied. There are many different types of fixings and fittings.
1 Standard stick pin, common until 1945
2 Lapel stud fixture
3 Standard wire brooch fitting in use since 1900 and common since 1945
4 Gilt or best brooch fitting, solid back
5 Solid backed safety-pin fixing—Tufty Club badge
6 Wire brooch on a lithograph back
7 White and Lambert crimped badge which disposes of the ring altogether. 'Badges are beautiful' was printed on card—solid backs in the late 1970s
8 White and Lambert 1¼ in (32 mm) with crimps, one a Westfield advertising paper insert—W & L make up button badges for Westfield although Westfield do their own plastic badges
9 Standard wire brooch, most of which are supplied to the trade by Whitecroft and Scovill of Lydney
10 London Badge Shop design of 1977
11 to **13** Manufacturers' badges: The Universal Button Company and the London Emblem Company are two of the biggest manufacturers in the country. They also sell hand-operated machines. The ring on Universal badges (*11*), and those made up on their machines, is normally more rounded giving the badge a thinner appearance when viewed from above, than the London Emblem badge (*12*). Also many of the 2¼ in (57 mm) designs in this book were made up by Universal as London Emblem (and others) opt for 2⅛ in (55 mm).
14 Moulded plastic ring as applied by B Sanders and Sons of Bromsgrove
15 to **20** Solid backs on a variety of badges made since 1977
16 and **17** Baynham and Stanfield *16* succeeding *17*, the inner ring clip, around 1981
18 to **20** Square and rectangular designs. Sanders' plastic solid back (*19*) succeeded the tin solid back around 1984. The original 'oblong' design was registered by Tony Fattorini of South Wales Badge Company around 1980. Parts for square and oblong designs are supplied to many firms in the UK and Europe by B Sanders and Sons of Bromsgrove

ring in was also an extra stage in the process. White and Lambert use a machine which bends the shell back on itself to crimp the bonded acetate to the shell. The 'crimps' come in sizes of 1 in (25 mm), $1\frac{1}{4}$ in (32 mm), $1\frac{1}{2}$ in (38 mm), $1\frac{3}{4}$ in (45 mm), $2\frac{1}{4}$ in (57 mm) and 3 in (77 mm). On the $2\frac{1}{4}$ in (57 mm) and 3 in (77 mm) a wire brooch fixture was not possible without the support of a ring, so a solid back of card with a pin fitting in the centre was adopted. For a period their solid backs held the slogan 'Badges are beautiful'. In 1985 White and Lambert were absorbed by W O Lewis (Badges Ltd), manufacturers of enamel badges, who continue to produce button badges.

Moulded backs

B Sanders and Sons of Bromsgrove were also dissatisfied about the tin rings. In 1973 they introduced a moulded ring, which was developed eventually to include a moulded plastic solid back for round, square and rectangular shells. On their rectangular badges is the registered number 988112. This design came from Tony Fattorini. Fattorini was employed by the South Wales Badge Company, which was eventually taken over by Bristol Buttons (West Country Marketing), and it was this firm that let Sanders use the design. B Sanders also sell the parts for these badges to other producers. They were first produced around 1980.

In 1973 a former member of Sanders staff set up The Button Badge Company of Kidderminster which soon became a large manufacturing concern. Within three years a member of the Button Badge Company left to set up his own company next door! This was Baynham Presswork, later Baynham and Stanfield. In 1976 they were fortunate enough to acquire the Mr Men contract, and the millions of these badges that sold must have helped to get Baynhams off the ground. Baynham Presswork also had ideas about solid backs, their 'inner ring clip design' being a step in this direction. By 1984 a moulded plastic solid back was introduced with a safety pin. This has PAT APP No 8309382 and REG Design APP No 1012837 on the back of the $2\frac{1}{8}$ in (55 mm) version.

Although one can distinguish and identify manufacturers of button badges by such tell-tale signs, it must always be remembered that they are not usually responsible for the design. Customers, such as advertising agencies, may supply their own designs. Throughout this book, when a manufacturer is mentioned alongside a badge, it does not necessarily mean the firm designed the badge. Indeed a design can be found to have been made up by two or even three manufacturers.

Badge detectives even look closely at the ring to help them distinguish manufacturers. One of the longest established producers, the Universal Button Company, were still using metal rings in 1985, as were the London Emblem Company and, although it is possible to over-generalize, the Universal ring is usually more rounded and bulbous than that of the London Emblem Company. Moreover Universal's prints are normally laminated whereas London Emblems are not.

The rise of the homemade badge

In the same way that the Mr Men helped Baynham Presswork, in 1975 the Wombles helped the London Emblem Company. This firm estimate that they sold three million Womble designs, helping to

Types of button badge design

Different shapes, different designs, different messages—button badges suit a wide variety of uses. 'Homemade' designs (*12* to *16*) have become widespread since 1977.

1 and **2** Prewar celluloid advertising mirrors, made in the same way as badges, but with a mirror back instead of a pin
3 Rainbow badge, 1985
4 British oval design, 1929
5 Heat-sensitive square button badge, 1985
6 Button badge on a whisky dispenser
7 F W Hannah key ring badge, 1984
8 A Clarks Commandos lithograph of 1970, stamped off centre. Lithographs are printed on a massive sheet of metal and stamped out
9 A set of 'button' button badges, possibly early 1970s
10 and **11** Star Wars flashing designs of 1983–4. The rear of the badge illustrates the microcircuit; a simple rubber toggle on the pin cuts the circuit when the badge is not in use
12 Wham badge earrings, 1984
13 A badge recalling that infamous punk group 'Frank and the Furters' 1978
14 A cheerful message for a Loughborough Church group for the under-fives, 'Little people'
15 A hand-painted design on top of another badge
16 A badge produced for the York Archaeological Trust newsletter

establish them as a large manufacturer. Outworkers were employed to help cope with orders, and they used hand-operated machines.

By 1977–78 the wider potential of the hand-operated machine was realized. More and more local groups wanted their own badges, often in small quantities. The larger manufacturers would not normally handle an order under 500, so the solution was the sale of hand-operated machines to local community groups for the production of their own badges. At £250 a machine was seen as a good investment, and badge components were £30 per 1,000. The onset of the 'homemade' button badge began.

Many groups who purchased machines, developed good printing techniques, and their badges are of a correspondingly good quality. Others, however, used photocopies or poor quality drawings. While many 'homemades' are of local or novelty interest, and are relatively rare because of the small quantities in which they are produced, they are not seen as being very collectable.

The use of hand-operated machines has affected the main manufacturers to some extent, although, clearly, anyone who wants a lot of over 1,000 badges will usually use a main manufacturer. Hand-operated machines have been sold in large numbers by the Universal Button Company, Enterprise Products and the London Emblem Company who also supply parts for badge assembly.

Novelty badges

The button badge boom of the late 1970s brought with it several innovations, one of which was the glitter or reflective badge. A crop of these emerged in 1980, only to disappear again. Other oddities such as heat-sensitive badges and liquid-crystal badges have also appeared. Similarly, micro-electric button badges (YES!) produced initially in America, have proved popular but expensive gimmicks. Apart from 'Happy Birthday' and 'Merry Christmas' designs, a set of electronic badges was produced in 1983 featuring Star Wars spacecraft with flashing lights.

Button badges have also been used to advertise alcohol in new ways. Apart from fixing a badge to a bottle opener, McNish Whisky stuck two on either side of their dispensers!

More recently, in 1984, two Wham $\frac{3}{4}$ in (19 mm) pop badges were fitted with a solid back and pin arrangement which made them into earrings—literally pin-on badges. Also in 1984, Rainbow Designs issued their $1\frac{1}{2}$ in (38 mm) Noddy set as 'magnet backs' for use on noticeboards and such like.

Enamel and metal badges

History and development

Enamel badges or brooches date back to before the Christian era, examples being found in Egyptian tombs. They were made by placing various shades of enamel into sections made by copper wire on base metal. These were then fired to make animal or floral patterns and the technique later became known as *cloisonné*. It was in the late eighteenth and early nineteenth century that enamelling of such articles began in England, centred mainly on Wednesbury in Staffordshire.

In Birmingham in the 1840s, the die-stamping machine was developed. This enabled dies to be struck with raised retaining lines, like the original *cloisonné* articles. However, as this process was much cheaper than the hand-printed method, the trade at Wednesbury virtually died.

It was not until the end of the nineteenth century that badges were made in any quantity. The emergence of clubs and societies and the beginning of seaside holidays and tourism, with a demand for souvenirs, was a boost for the manufacturers.

During the First World War many badges of flags of the allies and regiments were manufactured but after the war trade slumped dramatically. It began recovering in the 1930s when publicity badges and a vogue for collecting began.

Since 1945, as well as the original club badges, souvenirs and publicity items, there has been a steady growth in products for direct sale to the public, such as football emblems, cars, motorcycles and railway locomotives.

The manufacturing process

Making the die

Manufacture of a badge today begins with an actual-size coloured drawing for the customer to inspect. After approval the die-sinker cuts the outline on plastic sheet. This is enlarged five times so all the details are included, wherever possible. The outline is then transferred by a reducing pantograph machine to the face of the actual soft metal die and the appropriate areas cut away. The lines and letters that will appear in metal on the badge are flush with the surface, and the areas to contain the enamel are recessed and matted. When finished, the die is heat-treated and hardened.

The die is now ready to receive the blank metal for stamping. The blank is placed by hand onto the die, and a manually assisted drop stamp is operated or, for vast quantities, a hydraulic press is used.

Making the blanks

The blanks are made from gilding metal, which is composed of 90 per cent copper and 10 per cent zinc. Any more zinc and it would melt during firing, and if it was pure copper the darkening during heating would affect the transparent enamels such as red.

One of the chief suppliers of gilding metal is B Mason and Sons of Wharf Street, Birmingham. This firm has been producing metals since 1852 and their works backs onto the canal, where the raw materials used to be transported.

They prepare the gilding metal by mixing the copper and zinc in a two-ton electric induction furnace heated to 1100°. Samples are then tested for impurities and for hardness. When satisfactory the metal is poured into a holding vat from whence it is sent to a machine and set into a strip $\frac{3}{16}$ in (13 mm) by $1\frac{1}{2}$ in (38 mm). It is then moved to the rolling mill where it is reduced to the required thickness to within $\frac{2}{10}$ of a thousandth-inch.

After the blanks have been stamped, they are ready for clipping. Clipping is the removal of excess metal from the border of the badge, achieved by the use of a fly (hand) press or by a mechanical press which punches out the shaped badge. The scrap metal is recycled and the badge is ready to receive its fittings.

Fittings to hold the pins on the back are soldered in place on the stampings. These are cleaned in acid ready for enamelling.

Enamelling

Enamelling can be carried out in two ways, either by the traditional vitreous method or by the modern method of cold enamelling. Vitreous enamelling involves mixing crushed glass with water and a colour pigment. This mixture is scraped on to the blank in the required position. It is then put into a pre-heated unit at a temperature of 800°C until the enamel fuses to the metal. A hand-held gun may also be used to heat the enamel. Cold enamelling uses coloured epoxy which is applied to the area required, and put into an oven at 100°C for one hour. Epoxy can dry on its own, but the oven is used to speed up the process so that other colours may be added.

With either method only two different colours can be applied at the same time; between firings the surface has to be cleaned with acid so that the subsequent colours will fuse properly (this preparation is called linnishing). At this stage the letters or lines cannot be seen, and the badge looks somewhat lumpy. It is then carefully ground to remove the enamel from the metal areas until the surface is flat. The badge is fired once more to remove the scratch marks from the enamel. Finally, the pins are inserted and the metal areas polished on a circular electric mop to smooth the grinding scratches. Once the metal areas have been electroplated in chromium or gilt finish, the badges are ready for inspection and despatch.

Fittings

There are two basic pin attachments on enamel badges: a single fitting or a twin-mounted fitting. Single fittings include stick pins, lapel studs, screw studs, and 'pinched clip' studs. Twin-mounted fittings comprise a variety of safety-pin and brooch-pin attachments. A study for the Badge Collectors Circle identified well over 70 different fitting attachments, within these two basic types.

Enamel badge manufacturers

Enamel badges as we recognize them today became popular in the late nineteenth century when methods of stamping improved, and demand increased, stimulated by a variety of new clubs and societies. Many of the firms producing the badges predate this era by many

Early enamel badges

'Britain's Best Badges' as shown in the Thomas Fattorini Ltd 1927 catalogue. The range and quality of enamelled badges produced before the Second World War is evident. 'Please note the THOMAS in our name, as similar firms are NOT the same' was clearly to distinguish Thomas Fattorini Ltd from Fattorini and Sons.

BRITAIN'S BEST BADGES
FOR EVERY PURPOSE.

No matter what the requirement may be we can supply the suitable Badge, and will gladly submit a design for your exclusive use.

Cricket, Tennis, Bowling, Golf, Swimming, Harriers, Shooting, Rowing, Hockey, Football, Billiards, Cycling and Motor Cycling Clubs have all bought Badges from us.

Delegates Badge for wear at conferences, etc.

BRANCH CHAIRMAN

H.R.H. the Prince of Wales wore one of these Badges.

W1
Made with name for practically any official.

We supply Schools, Trades Unions, Political Associations, Social Clubs, Ambulance & Red Cross Societies, etc., and make Motor Radiator Plates & Advertising Badges and similar productions.

THOMAS FATTORINI
BADGES DO
INCREASE MEMBERSHIP.

Several members of the ROYAL FAMILY have been presented with and have worn Thomas Fattorini Badges— Please keep our name for reference.

THOMAS FATTORINI LIMITED
TRAFALGAR WORKS   Hockley Street   BIRMINGHAM.

Directors:
Thomas Fattorini
Frank Fattorini

Established over 100 Years.

Telegrams : "Enthusiasm."
Telephone : Central 261
Birmingham

Please note the THOMAS in our name, as similar firms are NOT the same.

13

years. Most are jewellers producing high quality goods who have specialized in badges, medals and insignia.

Fattorini badges

One such firm is Thomas Fattorini Ltd. The name Fattorini has appeared on badges (and medals) from the second half of the nineteenth century to the present day. Two branches of the family, one based in Bradford and the other in Skipton, traded independently for over 150 years until, in 1983, Thomas Fattorini Ltd of Skipton acquired Fattorini and Sons Ltd.

Both Thomas Fattorini Ltd and Fattorini and Sons Ltd started as retail jewellers making simple badges and medals in their workshops. When demand increased they bought stock from manufacturing jewellers in Birmingham and London. It was customary for these manufacturing jewellers to inscribe the badges with the name and hallmark of the retail shop if desired. For this reason it is impossible to determine which early items were made on Fattorini's premises. Around the time of the First World War both companies acquired factories in Birmingham. From that time on, either the Birmingham addresses were added or the addresses of the retail shops.

The following inscriptions are found:

Fattorini and Sons, Bradford: c1613–1916 (This shop retained the Fattorini name until the mid-1960s when the jewellers Samuels took it over.)
Fattorini and Sons, Bar Street, Birmingham: c1916–1983
I Fattorini, Skipton: c1886
T Fattorini, Skipton: c1886–1934
T Fattorini, Preston: 1903–1928 (Shop)
T Fattorini, Hockley Street, Birmingham: c1916–1927
T Fattorini, Regent Street, Birmingham: 1927 to the present
Frank Fattorini, Birmingham (A small concern that broke away from Fattorini and Sons and ceased trading c1970; exact dates unknown)
A Fattorini, Harrogate: 1931 (A shop, still trading, but not currently involved in making badges)

Other firms

The jewellery quarter of Birmingham is the centre for enamel and metal badge production in Britain, and many badges bear testimony to this by carrying the maker's name and address on the reverse of the badge, a clear bonus for collectors. Many of these firms are no longer in business. H W Miller Ltd who produced the first golly badges before the war, ceased trading in the early 1960s. John Pinches (London) who produced many early enamelled badges, were acquired by the Franklin Mint of America to make and market artistic medals. They ceased production of badges in the early 1970s. Several of the enamel and metal badge firms have had offices in both London and Birmingham, or moved from one place to the other.

The vast majority of producers hail from the Birmingham area. These include: AEW; The Birmingham Medal and Badge Company; Butler, Gladman and Norman; J R Gaunt Ltd; W O Lewis (Badges) Ltd; Manhattan Windsor Ltd; Marples and Beasley; Parry; T N Priest and Company; Vaughtons; W Reeves and Company; R E V Gomm; and Morton T Colver. Other notable names are The

Types of enamel badge backs

Makers' names often appear on the backs of enamel badges (*10* to *23*). Standard pin fixtures are most common (*10* to *23*).
1 Stages in the production of enamelled badges, from the blank of gilding metal to the stamping by a die and the clipping, followed by the soldering of pins on the rear
2 Lapel stud fixture by Thomas Fattorini Ltd
3 Lapel stud fixture by J R Gaunt, then of London
4 and **5** Screw stud fixtures
6 A safety clasp fixture
7 to **9** Stick pin fixtures
10 Thomas Fattorini Ltd, Regent St, Birmingham
11 W O Lewis (Badges) Ltd Birmingham. (For the NSPCC League of Pity)
12 Fattorini and Sons Ltd, Bradford Works, Birmingham
13 H W Miller Ltd, Branston St, Birmingham 15 (Dated 1947 for the Wilts County Tourists, The Moonrakers)
14 Reeves and Company, Birmingham
15 J R Gaunt, London
16 Morton T Colver, Birmingham
17 Marples and Beasley, Birmingham
18 W Reeves and Company, Birmingham
19 Davis Badge Company, London
20 R E V Gomm, Frederick St, Birmingham
21 Jewellery Company, Dublin
22 L Simpson and Company, London
23 Collins, London

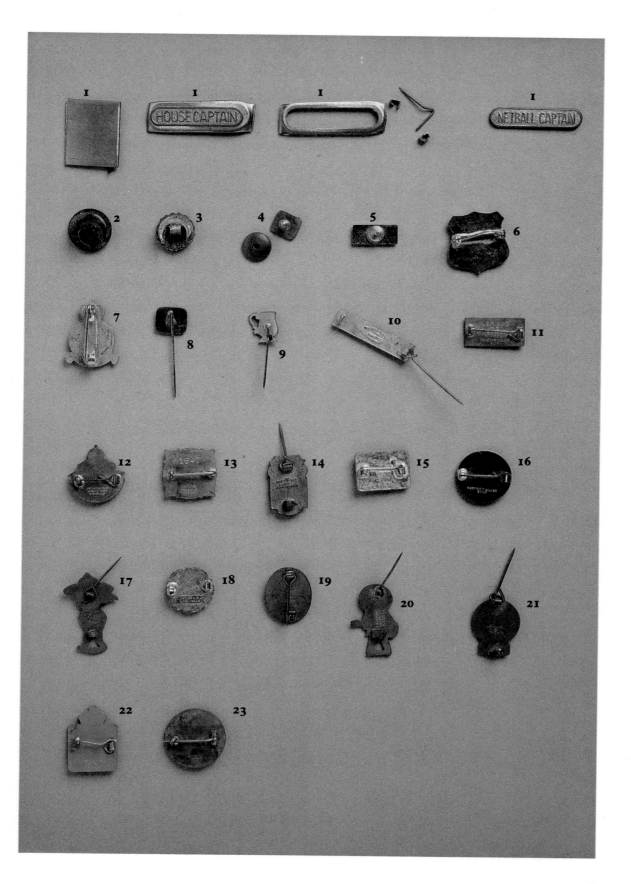

Jewellery Metal Company, Dublin; London Badge, London; L Simpson and Company Ltd, London; Coffer Ltd, London and Northampton; Firmin, London; Toye Kenning & Spencer, Warwickshire; and Collins, London. Most of these are still producing badges.

Other types of badges

Apart from button and enamel badges, badges have been made in a variety of other materials.
1 and **2** Printed card and leatherette badges
3 Thick gold-foiled leatherette badge
4 and **5** Card badges
6 and **7** Second-surface printed, mounted on formed metal disc with integral attachments
8 Second-surface printed insert on button badge-type back
9 and **11** Second-surface printed insert on plain back with formed attachments
10 Second-surface printed insert, mounted on a stamped background, 1984
12 Second-surface printed in formed insert
13 to **17** Paint-filled stamped badges
18 Formed metal badge, paint-filled
19 and **20** Printed stainless steel stamped out of a sheet
21 Printed metal stamped out of a sheet
22 A square button badge of sorts
23 Reverse printed glass mirror in plastic frame from around 1980

Other materials
Plastic, card, leatherette and imitation enamel

History and development

Apart from enamel and button badges, they are available in many other materials and in many other forms—from card and leatherette to wood and plastic. Many of these cheaper alternatives have proved damaging to the enamel badge trade in particular.

Card and leatherette

Card was an early alternative and, in the Universal Button Company catalogue of 1936, a gross of oval or round card badges with safety-pin backs was priced at 15 shillings. More ornately shaped card badges were also advertised, as were leatherette badges. Leatherette badges of 1¾ in (45 mm) diameter continued to be made for many years after the war, but by the 1970s they had been mainly superseded by plastic. The vast majority of card and leatherette badges were made for stewards and officials at conferences and exhibitions, although gold foiled leatherette place badges of 1¼ in (32 mm) diameter were being made in the late 1970s.

The hot foil printing process used on these leatherette badges, and on many plastic badges, is a direct descendant of the gold tooling found on early books. It is the only cheap way of fixing a perfect metallic colour, such as gold, silver or bronze, on to plastic, leather or wood, but is not suitable for use on metal since it relies on the use of heat to bond the design with the surface. Such badges are very resistant to abrasion.

Imitation enamel

Second-surface printing, or printing the underside of a transparent piece of plastic, is a method that has developed since 1945 but has only become commonplace during the 1970s. Its rapid growth has seen the demise of the enamel badge to some extent.

Most badges produced this way are 'inserted' on to a metal base, making them look like enamel badges. 'Second-surface printed' badges range from those printed on a more bulbous piece of clear plastic to those printed on a thinner acetate. Because of their cheapness they have caught on quickly; many are made in the Far East. Serious collectors, however, will have nothing to do with these 'imitations'.

Badges printed on stainless steel are now available. Printing on stainless steel would have been regarded as unsatisfactory in the 1960s, but it is now possible using heat-curing or ultraviolet-curing paints, or a mix of epoxy paints. Other metal badges include those issued by 'Lone Star' to junior sheriffs or detectives.

The stamped metal badge which is paint-filled rather than enamelled also became more popular in the late 1970s and early 1980s. Even classic badges such as Robertsons golly brooches have been acrylic-paint-filled instead of enamelled since 1980.

Plastic badges

Plastic lends itself to the creation of unusually shaped badges.
1 A Thomas Fattorini Ltd 'Universal Personal Badge'
2 Westfield Advertising 'Glowrim' badge—the rim is luminous
3 and **4** Westfield's moulded plastic paint-filled badges
5 to **10**, **12** and **16** Shaped moulded plastic badges, including Morph (6) an apt character for a moulded badge! 5, 9 and 10 are foil-tipped
11 Sawn acrylic sheet printed (Pontins Holiday Club)
13 Plastic hot foil stamped (Ford Amateur Club Golfers Home International Championships, 1981)
14 Part of a set of 'Stamp' badges from a punched plastic sheet, printed
15 A shaped pottery badge or brooch, 1975
17 Thomas Fattorini Ltd plastic design
18 Punched plastic sheet, printed
19 Thomas Fattorini Ltd plastic design

Around 1980 mirror badges became popular. Reverse-painted mirrors, often featuring pop stars, were usually inserted into a plastic frame complete with a pin fitting.

Plastic

Plastic badges have developed rapidly since 1945, although, interestingly, in 1923 Robertson's first-ever golly badge was made of a bakelite substance. Bakelite, developed in 1909 by Dr Leo Baekeland, was used for similar badges before the war, but these, like the golly, are extremely rare. It is ironic indeed that a plastic badge should be one of the most valuable.

The rapid development of plastics in the 1950s and 1960s gave rise to an increase in the use of the material for badges. Heat-shaped plastic badges appeared in the 1960s, such as the Esso man and World Cup Willie. Today injection moulding combined with foil tipping is responsible for many of the shaped plastic designs available.

With the advent of character merchandising in the 1970s, such badges featured everything from Mickey Mouse to Mr Men.

Other plastic badges are punched from a sheet or sawn from an acrylic sheet and printed. Some manufacturers have issued 'standard' plastic designs printed to suit customers' requirements.

Westfield Advertising of Birmingham have been making plastic badges for a number of years. Those worthy of mention include their 'Glowrim' badges with the names 'Rubyline' on the rear. These late 1970s plastic-backed designs have a print and plastic covering held in position by a luminous plastic rim. Westfield also produce an injection-moulded $1\frac{1}{2}$ in (38 mm) diameter fund-raising badge, in solid plastic with a safety-pin fixture. These badges, a cheaper alternative to the button badge, have proved popular with schools and clubs since their beginnings in 1978.

Name badges

Thomas Fattorini Ltd made badges for use at conferences and exhibitions, which displayed the name of the wearer and the company name, often in the form of company logo. Because these badges were heavy and expensive to make in metal, Fattorini decided that it would be a good idea to make a standard badge in plastic which could be printed with the permanent information and carry the name of the wearer on a card which could be typed or even handwritten. While this design was progressing it became apparent that many people objected to using pins on their clothing and that some form of clip was a desirable alternative. The design that evolved was a series of badges with common backs, the backs having both a pin and two clips. The fronts were in varying sizes, two being just simple frames to take a card, the other three with plain areas for printing. Patent application was made in 1970 and later granted and the individual designs were registered with the design registry.

These badges have proved to be very satisfactory. They can be produced economically and screenprinted in small quantities. More recently, with the advent of computer controlled engraving, plastic inserts have been used instead of card inserts. These are usually laminated and engraved so that the first colour shows through. For some time these 'Universal Personal' badges were exhibited at the Design Council.

When these badges were introduced there was a fairly general reluctance in Britain to wear name badges, and initially the bestselling badge was the smaller one. Now a custom is creeping in from the United States of identifying conference delegates with enormous badges, as large as 4 in by 2½ in (100 mm by 65 mm). The first name or nickname of the delegate appears in huge letters, enabling one to greet a total stranger across the room.

The Royal Family (from 1897)

Victorian and Edwardian designs

Badges celebrating royal events are very British, worn with pride by those who like to beat the patriotic drum. Various sorts have been produced for all the major royal events since 1897. However, not all celebrate such occasions in the same way. As the anti-royal lobby developed, from the 1960s onwards, so too did anti-royal badges.

The majority of designs in this section are of the button type—a good collection of royal badges reveals much about the development of button badges in Britain. Moreover they are seen as collectable by general collectors of royal regalia and so are quite sought after. Because of this, they are often over-priced by dealers although they are not particularly rare.

For manufacturers a royal event is a big money-spinner. Many enamel badges have also been produced for the various jubilees and coronations, often very decorative and looking more like medals.

1897 Diamond Jubilee

In 1897 button badges were just coming on the scene. Although it is hard to imagine Queen Victoria wearing one, she may have been amused to see the latest craze from America. The Diamond Jubilee button badges are among the very first, if not the first, issued in Britain. They were all made in the United States and shipped over, the Whitehead and Hoag Company of New Jersey being the manufacturers. Few examples are known. Most have the standard Whitehead and Hoag paper insert in the back including the patents, but the coloured badge complete with dates does not. It carries the name of the London agent – Lawrence – and Whitehead and Hoag's London address. Examples of these, as of many other royal badges, can be seen in the Museum of London.

Victoria 1898–1901

A variety of other Victorian button badges exist, most of which were made in the United States. A few were issued during the Boer War. On Victoria's death in 1901 button badges, bearing the words 'In Loving Memory', were issued, pinned to the centres of black shields.

Edward VII Coronation 1902

After the long sober reign of Victoria came to an end Edward VII revived the splendid public ceremonial of the monarchy. This is reflected to some extent in the badges produced in 1902 for his coronation. There are several colourful examples. One came complete with a rosette and has an interesting insert in the back, which reads, 'God save the King and Queen made in the USA'. Clearly the King and Queen were not made in the USA, but most of the button badges for their coronation were.

Early royal badges

Many early royal badges were imported from the United States.
1 to **6** Whitehead and Hoag imports from the United States, among the first button badges issued in Britain, together with their paper inserts
7 A celluloid button or badge believed made in Britain, and issued as a set of pin-back buttons
8 and **9** 1902 coronation import and its paper insert
10 to **12** Whitehead and Hoag standard 1902 design (*12*) complete with paper insert advert (*11*), and adapted for advertising (*10*)
13 to **17** Edward and Alexandra badges, probably made in Britain. *13* bears the name W and D Downey

1   2   3   4   5   6

7   8   9

10   11   12   13

14   15   16   17

The Whitehead and Hoag Company issued a standard design which could be adapted to suit the customer's needs. From such examples it is clear that the advertising potential of the button badge was already being recognized. Some feature an advert such as 'Scales and Sons Ltd for Best Wearing Boots' around the King and Queen design. These may have been given away or sold for a penny, as were others which contained an advert on the paper insert.

The influx of badges from the United States for the 1902 coronation helped to spark off manufacture in Britain. One 1902 coronation design which is thought to have been made in England shows the King in colour in his coronation gown. This badge bears the words 'W & D Downey copyright' on the rim and is believed to have been made by a button manufacturer. Other 1902 designs are also believed to have been made in Britain on button-making equipment. In fact, some are believed to have been issued as buttons.

George V and Edward VIII

George V

The two major royal events in the reign of George V were his coronation in 1911 and Silver Jubilee in 1935. By 1911 the influx of American badges had stopped, and button badges were being produced in Britain. Several of the 1911 examples bear a copyright and are colourful and eye-catching. The use of flags, inset photographs and gold colouring around the edges gives the designs a regal splendour.

For the Jubilee in 1935 the most common designs were lithographs, printed directly onto tin, and the lack of colour gives these badges a more mundane look. The fact that they were lithographs means that they were probably made in great numbers (tens of thousands if not hundreds of thousands), and probably sold for a halfpenny or penny each. One 1935 badge that was given away with soap bears the words 'Souvenir of the Silver Jubilee 1935'. This badge has a paper insert in the back which reads, 'Gossages 1d Dry Soap still the best'.

Edward VIII

Edward VIII only reigned from January to December 1936. No doubt in 1936 badge manufacturers were very busily planning for 12 May 1937, the date set for the coronation. Edward VIII was very popular with the people and manufacturers were anticipating a brisk trade. When the King abdicated in order to marry Mrs Simpson, a divorced woman, many of these stocks must have been scrapped.

Many of the badges have disappeared without trace, although some have since turned up, sold in bulk to retailers, or found in manufacturers' warehouses. In the 1936 catalogue, Thomas Fattorini shows many Edward VIII coronation souvenirs. Apart from the many medals featured, there are two enamel badges and a button badge. Enamels sold at 12 shillings per dozen, and the button badge (referred to as a celluloid badge) cost £5-5-0 per thousand with a stick pin or £5-15-0 with wire or brooch fitting.

Similarly, the Universal Button Company had in stock King Edward VIII photo buttons (pin backs) at nine shillings per gross $\frac{7}{8}$ in (23 mm) or 18 shillings per gross $1\frac{1}{4}$ in (32 mm). Clearly these were not just for the coronation. Edward VIII was so popular with the people that he warranted a stock of button badges.

George V to Edward VIII

Many of these designs are lithographs (*11, 12, 16, 18, 19, 20*), implying that vast numbers were produced.

1 to **5** George V coronation designs, 1911

6 to **12** George V Silver Jubilee designs, 1935, including one with an advert insert (*8*)

13 to **20** Edward VIII designs, many for the coronation which did not take place. *17* consists of unprotected paper in a metal frame

George VI and Queen Elizabeth II

George VI

One manufacturer was determined to brighten things up in 1937 and for the coronation of George VI produced the 'Litbadge'—'the only illuminated badge made'. One cannot help but think this idea came from America, but it does say 'Made in England' on the box! (The lamp was foreign-made). These retailed for sixpence and if you could afford the torch batteries to go with it you must have been the envy of all your school pals in those dark days of the 1930s. These badges are not particularly common which indicates that not too many were sold. Powered badges didn't reappear until the 1970s (although several luminious badges were produced between these dates).

Several other designs, both enamel and button badges, were produced in 1937. One for the Co-op is in green and yellow—unusual colours for a royal design. The much sought-after coronation golly, produced by H W Miller of Birmingham for Robertson's jam, was also issued in 1937. This brooch is revered by golly collectors and shows golly saluting with a white gloved hand. He wears a Union Jack waistcoat instead of the normal yellow one.

Queen Elizabeth II Coronation

The designers of coronation badges in 1953 saw the Queen and Prince Philip almost as film stars—judging by a set of two that shows their majesties looking more like Bob Hope and Dorothy Lamour. Staying with cinema, the ABC Minors Cinema Club produced a badge for the coronation in splendid red, white, blue and gold. A colour lithograph of flags formed a backdrop for Her Majesty, whose lipstick is as vivid as her jewellery. In sharp contrast the standard designs for 1953 are much more sober and respectable.

George VI to Queen Elizabeth II

The straightforward photographic treatment of the 1977 Jubilee designs compares favourably with the more fanciful 1953 efforts.
1 The 1937 'Litbadge' complete with box, bulb and wire
2 A colourful 1937 Co-op design
3 to **6** Other George VI coronation designs
7 Teddy Tail League with coronation bar of merit, made by Thomas Fattorini Ltd. There was also a coronation golly badge in 1937
8 and **12** Glamorous designs for the coronation of 1953. *8* is a lithograph
9 A youthful Queen
10, **13**, **14**, and **15** The official coronation designs
11 ABC Minors Cinema Club coronation design
16 to **18** Photographic set for the 1977 Silver Jubilee

Silver Jubilee 1977

One small irony of the 1977 Silver Jubilee is that many people were wearing badges stating 'The King is Dead'. The King, of course, was Elvis Presley, whose death coincided not only with the Silver Jubilee but also with the badge explosion that accompanied punk rock. The premier punk rock group, The Sex Pistols, whose notorious record 'Anarchy in the UK' was at the top of the charts summed up current feeling with a badge saying 'God Save the Sex Pistols', a design that also points to the shrewd timing of their manager, Malcolm Mclaren. Perhaps even more than in the swinging sixties youth culture was responsible for a massive increase in the turnover of badges.

Clearly a royal celebration was another reason for the upsurge in badges. It had been 24 years since the last royal occasion and people were ready for flag-waving and nationalistic fervour. But with the emergence of the National Front highlighting the bad side of patriotism, anti-royal feeling was also much in evidence. The Universal Button Company, who made vast quantities of Jubilee badges, estimated that for every ten Jubilee badges they made one saying 'Stuff the Jubilee'.

Many companies found the Jubilee was a good excuse for a bit of advertising, including Able Jack DIY Stores, Masons Pop and Olympus cameras. On the sporting front, Ladbroke Stadium among others issued a badge. London Zoo and Whipsnade Park weren't going to be left out either and issued badges featuring a monkey, which in the light of the anarchists' designs was a brave thing to do. Butlins holiday camp also produced a Silver Jubilee badge, although the days of their ornate enamels had long since past, and this was a printed insert stuck into a metal formed back.

There were several galas, fairs and street parties for which badges were made (mostly professionally as the days of 'homemades' were in their infancy). Pre-school playgroups and Scouts' organizations also issued badges—the scouting one being an enamel.

Charity, too, was to be found among the 1977 badges. The Silver Jubilee appeal founded by the Prince of Wales had a badge depicting Charles with the words 'Helper of the Prince of Wales'. Further badges associated with this appeal were also issued, such as the Silver Jubilee Appeal Greenwich badge.

There are more than 10 official Jubilee designs, produced in several sizes. Straight Union Jack badges were made in six sizes by various companies. One of these also features the Queen's head and dates. A photo-set of three 2¼ in (57 mm) badges also appeared, improvements on the film star look of 1953. Several designs were issued with the official logo, and a standard photo of the Queen on a white background with flags was issued in five sizes. A novelty badge used a 5p piece held in place with acetate, to show the Queen's head. I wonder how many children who were given this badge later broke the acetate to spend the 5p!

In 1977 Kojak (played by Telly Savalas) was a television favourite and his catchphrase 'Who loves ya baby' adorns a badge stating 'She is the greatest'. Another badge carries the slogan 'The Queen rules O K', a play on the popular modern graffiti.

1977 Silver Jubilee

The Jubilee coincided with a 'badge boom'. Badges produced for the event cover the whole spectrum of opinion.

1 Design with 5p piece held between the print and the acetate. One wonders how many children broke open the badge for the coin!

2, 5 and **6** Standard designs. *5* is a lithograph, *6* is by White and Lambert

3 The 'Rules O K' slogan became common in England in 1975 with the 'Free George Davis' campaign. It originated in Northern Ireland in the 1970s

4 Scouting movement enamel design

8, 9 and **12** Designs for parties and discos celebrating the Jubilee

10 A Kojak-inspired slogan

11 A second-surface printed insert Butlins badge for the 1977 Jubilee

13 Pre-school Playgroups Association design

14 and **15** The Silver Jubilee appeal had raised £13,000,000 by the end of 1977. These are just two badges which helped

16 Plastic foil-tipped badge

17 and **21** Designs from the 'Movement against a Monarchy'. London Transport announced they were going to re-name the Fleet line underground as the Jubilee line. A badge was produced, by the Movement against a Monarchy, stating 'Fleet line don't Jubilee've it'. Another badge produced by Movement against a Monarchy showed the Queen in caricature and asserted 'We won't stand for the National Anthem'.

18 The Sex Pistols were celebrating anarchy in 1977

19 and **20** Two 'Stuff the Jubilee' designs. *19* was by the Socialist Workers Party

Charles and Diana—The Royal Wedding 1981

Although only four years elapsed between 1977 and 1981, much had happened politically to affect the design of the Royal Wedding badges. The ugly face of nationalism, in the form of the National Front, had reared its head and a big anti-fascism pressure group had developed along with many anti-racism groups. The use of the Union Jack by the National Front tended to tarnish it somewhat. It is certainly true to say that the 1981 designs show far fewer flags than ever before and those flags that are depicted are much less prominent.

Many designs incorporated the official photographs, and these can be found in several sizes and with various styles of print around them. Colourmaster, a button badge producer mostly of 'places' badges, issued two official badges which were coded BX969a and BX969b. A set of three rectangular designs was also issued and are quite sought after for their different appearance. One of the nicest 1981 badges is one of the few which does not depict the couple in their official guise. It shows their faces inset in a heart shape and Charles looks as though he has just finished playing polo, while Diana looks like a schoolgirl.

With the popularity of Charles, and the public's happy anticipation of the wedding, protest badges were not quite so evident in 1981. Socialist Unlimited did produce a 'Stuff the Wedding' badge which sold quite well. Others included 'Don't do it Di' produced by Spare Rib, the feminist magazine, and '29 July General Strike against the Monarchy' produced by Fly Press.

The best badge of 1981, however, has to be 'The King and Di' which shows Charles with a bald head à la Yul Brynner. It is the ears that make this badge so funny, plus the fact that you know Charles would more than likely approve, with his Goonish sense of humour.

1981 Royal Wedding

This royal occasion inspired another range of alternative 'anti' designs (*15* to *19*).

1 to **3** A set of rectangular button badges
4 Badges for royal visits in Britain are quite rare
5, 6, 7, 9, 10, and **14** Designs using the official photographs; *7* is by Colourmaster, *10* by Rainbow Designs
8 A heart design showing Princess Diana looking like a schoolgirl
11 and **12** Designs with flags were unusual in 1981
15 Charles as Yul Brynner
16 Socialist Workers Party 'Stuff the Wedding' design
17 'The Windsor Zoo', another 'anti' design
18 'Don't do it Di' by Spare Rib
19 '29th July General Strike against the Monarchy!' by Fly Press

Politics

It was not until the 1960s and 1970s that political badges became common in Britain. However, the value of badges in campaigns was soon realized in the United States. In 1896, the same year button badges were invented, they were used in the McKinley versus Bryan presidential election, and they have been popular in America ever since.

After 1960, the number of badges produced in support of various campaigns is so great that they have been grouped here in separate sections, according to theme.

1896 to 1918

Boer War

In Britain, the button badges issued during the Boer War are among the first that appeared here. Once again, as with the Diamond Jubilee in 1897, badges were imported from the United States, from Whitehead and Hoag of Newark, New Jersey. There are a great number and variety of these. The majority are $\frac{7}{8}$ in (22 mm) diameter and feature a portrait photograph on a white background, with the name underneath. Others include flags and some are in colour.

Apart from these imports, many other examples exist that have a simple photograph design but no writing. Although no maker's name is shown, these are believed to have been produced by British button manufacturers, and they may in fact be the first home-produced button badges. One such manufacturer was B Sanders and Sons of Bromsgrove. They are certain they produced a range of Boer War badges featuring generals, but unfortunately all such samples would have been destroyed in a fire at the factory in 1958. It is thought that most of the badges were sold for a penny each to raise funds for the war effort. The American badges were probably issued from 1899 to 1900, during the early part of the war, at which point British manufacturers seized the opportunity and produced their badges until the end of the war in 1902.

Although patriotic and imperialist sentiments ran high at the turn of the century, the war was not altogether popular, and many, including Lloyd George, had sympathy for the Boers. This is probably why Whitehead and Hoag also produced badges showing President Krueger. Irish republicans, too, sympathized with the Boers; the National Museum of Ireland in Dublin has 11 pro-Boer badges, mostly showing Krueger.

The exact purpose of these Boer War designs is not altogether clear. They may have been sold to raise funds for the war, or sold as part of a campaign to popularize the war. It has also been suggested that they were used to decorate soldiers when metal for medals was in short supply.

Early political badges

Like the royal issues, most early political badges were imported from the United States. A number of designs were produced in Britain during the First World War (27 to 36).

1 to **7** Whitehead and Hoag of Newark, New Jersey produced these designs which were issued in Britain during the Boer War. The National Museum of Ireland in Dublin has 11 pro-Boer designs which were worn by Irish sympathizers (1)

8 to **20** Boer War designs believed to be made in Britain. The variation in production indicates that several British button manufacturers were making these, although no makers' names appear. 10 came complete with celluloid rosette. Known generals are General Buller (8) and (13), General Lord Kitchener (9), Field Marshall Lord Roberts VC (10, 11 and 15), Colonel Baden-Powell (12), General French (14), Gatacre (16), Methuen (17), General Sir George Stewart White (18 and 19)

21 This Boer War design featuring Andy Wauchope bears the words Requiescat in Pace, 'Rest in Peace'

22 to **26** All believed to be politicians. 23 has the paper insert stating, 'Liberals support your own press—buy only the Yorkshire Evening News' and was probably for the 1910 election

27 A badge by UPB Co, London

28 Design showing the royal standard

29 and **30** Designs featuring flags of the allies; 29 has the name Forman of Nottingham on the curl

31 A design by Fattorini, Bradford

32 A war bond badge

33 and **35** Probably 'sweetheart' badges

1900 to 1918

From 1900 to 1914 the labour movement was transforming its economic strength into political power in the form of the Labour Representation Committee. In 1900, 1906 and 1910 this Committee (which became the Labour Party) forged election agreements with the Liberals and many badges appeared to support candidates. The progressive Liberal Press published these. In the northeast, the Northern Echo published 32 badges featuring candidates for the 1910 election. These were sold at one shilling for a card of 16 direct from the Echo, or a penny each from newsagents. Similar badges appeared elsewhere, such as those published by the Yorkshire Evening News in Leeds. It would appear that, right from the outset, button badges were largely to be the tool of the Labour movement rather than the right-wing or establishment.

At the outbreak of war in 1914 the government needed to raise money for the war effort. Badges were given for £1 bonds sold as a 'memento of the Great European War'. Before the horrors of the trenches became common knowledge, many badges expressed patriotic fervour: 'Our Empire's War for the World's peace' is an example produced by U P B Company, London. Servicemen could also have their own badges made up for their sweethearts to wear. Another early supplier of British button badges was Forman of Nottingham, and their badge, 'Honour to whom Honour is due' shows the flags of the allies. Badges were also issued to civilians 'On war service'.

1918 to 1945

Between the wars

Button badges were produced for politicians of all parties at election times, with many enamels also being made for political associations. During this period there was much trade-union activity, which encouraged the production of many badges. Apart from the many union amalgamations that were taking place, the working-class struggle reached fever pitch with the 1926 General Strike and the hunger marches of the 1930s.

Right-wing associations also flourished in this period; their enamels are easier to find now than button badges. Conservative associations did produce some button badges, but usually chose enamels. The Primrose League, Imperial League and Unionist Association also adopted enamel badges, many of which were made in large numbers. Members of the Primrose League agreed to do their best to maintain Religion, the Constitution and the Honour of the British Empire. One particularly ornate Primrose League badge, made by W O Lewis, was double-sided and the centre of the badge swivelled so that it could be worn either way round. After the Second World War the Imperial League was reformed and became the Young Conservatives. Thus, any Young Conservative badges date from 1945 onwards. One interesting right-wing button badge features Joseph Chamberlain and states, 'Chamberlain day Follow our Joe's lead 1931'. Joseph Chamberlain had been a keen imperialist during his time in parliament at the beginning of the century. This badge must have celebrated an 'Empire Day' and probably emanated from the Imperial League.

Union badges

A selection of trade union enamelled badges produced by Thomas Fattorini Ltd, shown in their 1939 catalogue, indicates the rise in union activity between the wars. Thomas Fattorini Ltd was the biggest supplier of badges to trade unions.

TRADES UNION BADGES

Ask for a special design and quotation — it will be sent post free on request.

Badges made by Thomas Fattorini are noted for the brilliance of the enamel and beautiful finish.

Thomas Fattorini Ltd. have made hundreds of thousands of Enamelled Badges for Trades Unions and guarantee complete satisfaction to any Union placing its orders with them.

Miners' Safety Badges.

We have made and designed these Special Badges for many customers and will submit a special sketch for you without obligation.

THOMAS FATTORINI LTD. REGENT STREET WORKS **BIRMINGHAM, 1**

PLEASE NOTE THE **THOMAS** IN OUR NAME AS SIMILAR FIRMS ARE **NOT** THE SAME

Second World War

At the outbreak of the Second World War air-raid precautions were uppermost in many people's minds. Never before had the civilian population felt so vulnerable. Firms were encouraged to form groups of employees into ARP corps, while badge firms encouraged such volunteers to wear badges. These badges, many of them enamels, are quite sought after. Similarly, workers in munitions factories wore badges to show they were doing their bit. Such war service badges are often cruelly referred to as 'white feather badges'.

During the desperate struggle to produce aircraft, Spitfire funds were started all over the country, and many sold button badges to raise money. Thomas Fattorini made tens of thousands of badges for the numerous 'War Weapons Weeks' held during 1940 and 1941.

Another fascinating badge reads 'Blackpool Aids Russia', the result of local fund-raising. Mrs Churchill, with her 'Aid to Russia' flag days, was asking people to increase their penny a week to the Red Cross so that a proportion could be sent to Russia. Apart from producing many ARP badges, Thomas Fattorini Ltd also made luminous button badges in an attempt to help people through the blackout.

1945 to 1977

In 1945 it was V for Victory and many badges showing Churchill and his famous symbol were made. One design was a metal badge with a V and the slogan 'Send for Churchill'. This badge was issued in large quantities during the 1945 to 1950 Labour government. An advertisement in the Conservative Yearbook of 1951 offers the badge as a souvenir for two shillings post free. A salesman, one W B Smith, persuaded Sir Anthony Eden to wear one, which was quite an achievement as Eden had been 'waiting in the wings' for many years.

Through the 1960s the all-party debate on the Common Market raged until Prime Minister Heath finally signed the entry treaty. Nevertheless, in 1974 there was a referendum as to whether we should remain a member of the Common Market. A variety of designs were produced for both sides.

Politicians were fair game in the 1960s in the growing wave of anti-establishment feeling. 'Scilly Wilson' referring to Prime Minister Wilson's frequent holidays in the Scilly Isles is but one example. At the same time the 'I'm backing Britain' campaign was growing, for which many badges were made.

In the late 1960s hippies were making 'Love not war' and the 'Legalize cannabis' campaign had its roots. From 1977 onwards the making and selling of manual badge-making machines by the London Emblem Company among others, meant that small political groups could produce their own designs. Many of these groups also produced other 'homemades' for a variety of non-political causes. The quality of design was initially poor, but as expertise improved with use so did the quality of badges.

During the secrecy scandals of the late 1970s, people walked up and down Whitehall wearing badges with 'I'm a security risk', and 'Tell me your official secrets'.

Campaign badges

This selection includes designs for right-wing groups (*1* to *8*); wartime fund-raising (*9* to *13*); the Common Market debate (*15* to *19*); and official secrecy (*23* to *25*).

1 1920s design with insert of the Merchants Portrait Company, Kentish Town Road, London

2 and **3** Badges for Conservative Associations

4 and **5** The Imperial and Constitutional League became the Young Conservatives in 1945. Both badges were made by W O Lewis

6 and **7** Primrose League designs made by W O Lewis. The central section of *7* swivels to reveal the Primrose League logo on the other side

8 Chamberlain Day, for the politician Joseph Chamberlain, was probably connected with the Imperial League as Chamberlain had been a keen Imperialist at the turn of the century

9 to **11** Designs for the Spitfire Fund

10 A Thomas Fattorini Ltd design

12 Badge for Blackpool's Navy Week

13 Mrs Churchill organized an 'Aid to Russia' flag day during the war and this design is clearly connected

14 Produced by J R Gaunt of London to be worn by munitions workers. Thomas Fattorini Ltd produced many badges for wartime workers such as ARP volunteers

15 to **19** Badges for the Common Market debate of the 1960s and 1970s; *17* to *19* are White and Lambert crimps

20 and **21** 1960s free speech and civil liberty designs

22 Cannabis leaf and Rastafarian colours on the 'Legalise cannabis campaign' design

23 to **25** Badges relating to the secrecy scandals of the late 1970s. It was said that wearing 23 and 24 together constituted breaking the Official Secrets Act

1979 to 1985

Many political badges since 1979 feature Prime Minister Thatcher. By 1985 there were well over 200 different designs showing her, 99 per cent of these anti-Thatcher. One of the exceptions is the badge 'Love Maggie X' produced for her birthday and the 1979 election. The left followed this up with a caricature by Ralph Steadman stating 'Upset her, join the Labour Party', along with many varieties of 'Don't blame me I voted Labour'. 'I didn't vote Tory', and its variants were big sellers. It was the *Morning Star* newspaper that first issued this badge after Thatcher's 1979 election victory and within two months over 100,000 had been sold.

The Young Liberals were also active badge producers under the guise of 'liberator badges'. One of their best sellers was 'If Mrs Thatcher is the answer, it must be a silly question'. During the same period the Social Democratic Party was emerging. The SDP was seen by many as neither one thing nor the other; the design 'Keep politics out of politics join the SDP' was also popular.

The York Community Bookshop was one of an increasing number of outlets for political badges that appeared in the 1970s. They produced very comprehensive catalogues which are excellent guides for the collector. In 1980 their foresight led to the production of the 'Coming soon—1984' badge.

In 1977 the International Socialists of 26 years' standing assumed a new identity—the Socialists Workers Party (later called Socialists Unlimited)—and they were responsible for some of the best-designed political button badges of this period. In 1978 the 'Tea Pot Club' published an anti-government badge featuring Guy Fawkes and the slogan 'The only person to enter parliament with honest intentions'.

Through the early 1980s the volume of anti-Thatcher badges increased despite the Falklands War, and this provoked the Young Conservatives into producing badges, with such slogans as 'Socialist Worker a contradiction in terms'.

Despite the association of badges with left-wing protest, their use can also be a shrewd piece of private enterprise. This was demonstrated in 1981 when Tony Wedgwood Benn ran for deputy leader of the Labour Party. The Marxist weekly newspaper, *Socialist Challenge*, put up £779.80 for 15,000 badges to be printed in support of Mr Benn's campaign. John Silkin, one of the other candidates, appealed to Mr Benn to hold 'a democratic British election, not a Mafia-type American jamboree'. It was pointed out that if all 15,000 badges were sold at 25p each they would bring in around £3,000 profit. *Socialist Challenge* stated that they were not in it for the profit and that their motive was a political one.

The Falklands War of 1982 produced very few badges. The Falklands Islands office issued a badge simply stating 'Support the Falkland Islanders'. The *Sun* newspaper issued a badge saying, 'The Sun says good luck lads' while the York Community Bookshop produced three 'Troops Out' badges. A Falklands appeal was launched without a badge, but some of the resulting galas produced badges.

Protest badges

The badge is the perfect vehicle for political protest, whether on behalf of an official party or not.
1 In 1977 the International Socialists of 26 years' standing took on a new identity as the Socialist Workers Party. They were responsible for many cleverly designed badges from 1977 to 1985. 'Eat the rich' is a 1977 design
2 and **3** SWP anti-Thatcher designs published by Socialists Unlimited
4 and **8** Following the 1979 election many designs of this ilk were issued. *4* features a Ralph Steadman cartoon. Both are unusual in that the publishers' and printers' names appear on the face of the design
5 and **6** Two Communist Party of Britain Marxist-Leninist anti-Thatcher designs of early 1980s
7 Published by Fly Press
9 to **12** 1982 Falklands designs. *9* and *11* were produced by the York Community Bookshop; *10* is a rare patriotic design published by a service station; *12* is the *Sun* newspaper's badge issued when the first troops sailed
13 to **16** Slogans from George Orwell's book were used on this 1984 set, believed produced by an anarchist group
17 and **18** 1981–2 designs by the York Community Bookshop
19 1981 design for Tony Benn's campaign to be deputy leader of the Labour Party
20 David Steel, the Liberal leader, appears on this official Liberal Party badge
21 Right-wing badges such as this 1984 design are unusual
22 and **23** Badges of the early 1980s dismissing all parties— Tories as greedy; Labour as envious; and the SDP as the 'sitters on the fence'. *23* was published by Leeds Postcards in 1981

Trade union badges

Trade union badges are among the most collected outside uniform badges. From the development of trade unions in the 1890s to their many amalgamations up to the Second World War countless beautifully designed enamel badges were produced. Indeed, while button badges of non-union pressure groups best reflect the struggles of the left since the 1960s, it is the decorative enamels of trade unions that tell this story before that date. There are collections of trade-union badges in many museums; the TUC's official collection is huge.

The early trade-union designs of the nineteenth century are among the earliest political badges. Initially, when trade unions were illegal, it took great courage to wear the badge. Workers would sew them into their lapels revealing them only at union meetings. Later, badges were used to show that a member was paid up, and these were often issued quarterly. Although the vast majority are enamelled copper and brass, silver and gold were often used for long service or merit awards. Button badges also were not uncommon, and plastic was used.

From 1920 to 1980 the number of trade unions decreased as a result of amalgamations. The giant Transport and General Workers Union, for example, merged with 80 different unions during those 60 years. These amalgamations involved some obscure unions, such as the 'Scottish Horse and Motor Vans Association', and as sometimes only initials appear on the badge such finds can be bewildering—a good trade-union directory will come in handy here. The designs are very strong on symbolism. Two hands shaking is a popular design. Powerful slogans such as, 'Unity is strength', 'We are as one', 'Educate, organize, control', 'Defence not defiance' and 'The cause of Labour is the hope of the world' were adopted. Railwaymen have always been keen to show their allegiance by wearing their union badges. In the 1930s the NUR held 'badge weeks' to promote recruitment.

Campaign badges

Campaign badges have also been made in large numbers. Quite often these were 'victory' badges produced after successful strikes. After the 1919 railways strike, when the NUR and ASLEF stuck together, 'Solidarity won the railway strike' was the slogan on the badge.

Button badges have been increasingly used since the 1960s in trade-union struggles. During the 1971 campaign against the government's Industrial Relations Bill a massive union demonstration of over 100,000 marchers took place and thousands of 'Kill the Bill' button badges were worn. During a steel strike angry workers and residents actually threw button badges at Members of Parliament in the House of Commons shouting, 'Here's some steel from Corby.'

In 1984 the TUC produced badges commemorating 150 years of the Tolpuddle martyrs. One was enamel and one a button. The design on the button badge was based on an award-winning design from the 1934 centenary celebrations. In the same year, 1984, the miners began their long strike. The length of the strike and its intensity led to the production of hundreds of different badges. A few of these were enamels but most were button badges, many of which were 'home-made' by small groups for local collieries. One group—'Peace Action Durham'—raised well over £2,500 by selling over 20,000 such badges including at least 65 different designs.

Trade union badges

1 Early button badge of the National Amalgamated Union of Enginemen, Firemen, Mechanics, and Electrical Workers. One of over 80 unions which eventually merged with the TGWU
2 1929 Transport and General Workers Union button badge, showing the bearer as a paid up member
3 1930s National Union of Railwaymen button badge
4 and 5 Prewar button badges used for promotional purposes for the union homes
6 Amalgamated Union of Engineering Workers plastic badge for representatives, made by Thomas Fattorini Ltd
7 1970s Ford strike button badge
8 One of two badges produced to mark the Tolpuddle Martyrs 150th anniversary in 1984
9 Trades Union Congress design of 1979
10 'Keep Music Live' design of 1980, one of many issued during the musician's strike of that year
11 National Union of Public Employees badge against the cuts in public services, 1980–1
12 Transport and General Workers Union, modern enamel
13 Blackpool delegate's badge for 1983, for the Union of Shop, Distributive and Allied Workers
14 and 15 National Union of Railwaymen long-service badges. 14 was produced by Toye, Kenning and Spencer. 15 was produced by Thomas Fattorini Ltd and stamped 'Brothers in Unity'
16 1984–5 Miners' strike enamel produced for Markham Main colliery
17 to 29 Many badges supporting the miners' strike 1984–5 were made by local groups on their own machines; Peace Action, Durham produced at least 65 different designs. 19, and 21 to 30 are part of the PAD set which, apart from attacking Mr MacGregor (25 and 30), and working miners (29), also made use of popular characters such as Dennis the Menace (26), and the pop group Frankie Goes To Hollywood (22). 20 is a 1984 National Union of Railwaymen design for the Leicestershire town of Coalville, where railwaymen backed the striking miners even though most of the Coalville miners were working.
30 1984–5 General Municipal Boilermakers and Allied Trades Union button badge in support of local services against government cut-backs

International politics

Politicians

Before 1939, badges depicting the world's Communist and Fascist leaders were probably worn at great risk to life and limb, and are very rare. Since the 1960s, badges issued in Britain featuring international politicians, leaders and thinkers are not uncommon. Karl Marx is probably at the top of the list; there is even a 1980 design in glitter which shows him poking out a red tongue. Trotsky and Lenin, too, appear on many button badges. One badge has a portrait of Lenin as a boy in the centre of a red five-pointed star. The star is red transparent plastic set on to a shaped light alloy back.

Other favourites are Che Guevara, Ho Chi Minh, Mao Tse Tung, American black activists such as Malcolm X, and African leaders such as Haile Selassie, Jomo Kenyatta, Joshua Nkomo. American presidents, too, are not forgotten, although most of these badges are to do with the pacifist movement. Red and black stars have proved popular in enamel also, and other symbols such as the hammer and sickle are not uncommon.

Campaigns since the 1960s

In the 1960s, groups arose such as the Committee of 100, formed as a 'backlash' to the conservative leadership of the CND movement and its passive politics of that period. The Committee of 100 believed in more direct non-violent action such as sit-ins, and occupying air bases. Many famous names, such as Bertrand Russell, were associated with the Committee.

Campaigns such as Anti-Apartheid, Chile Solidarity, El Salvador Solidarity, Free Palestine and many others, were all during the 1970s and 1980s. The 1978 World Cup in Argentina provoked the badge 'Argentine football yes, torture no' and is typical of many badges attacking Fascism in South American countries. Lloyds Bank got some bad publicity in the 1970s when they were found to have secret dealings with Chile; the badge 'Avoid Lloyds, Lloyds funds Fascism in Chile' did not please them. Amnesty International, an organization for the release of political prisoners, produce several sizes of button badge featuring their logo. 'Russian tanks, no thanks' and 'Remember Czechoslovakia' are late 1970s designs. The Polish Solidarity Campaign resulted in several badges being issued in Britain in the early 1980s.

Northern Ireland

The Republicans in Ireland were among the first to use button badges when they fought against the British alongside the Boers. Since then they have issued designs covering all the major events. In the 1960s the message was 'One country'. As the troubles worsened in the 1970s 'Troops out now' was a slogan which became a movement. Various designs sold heavily. In 1980–82 H Block prisoners were at the centre of the troubles, and a group called Information in Ireland issued several designs, including 'Smash the H Blocks' and, as the hunger strikes worsened, 'Bobby Sands M.P. we remember'. 'Free all Irish Political prisoners' (published by Other Bookshops) and 'End internment in Ireland' were other early 1980s designs. The use of plastic bullets was another fiercely contested issue.

Badges have been worn in support of many international campaigns.
1 A design produced by Bangladesh Students Action Committee in 1972
2 1970s Anti-Apartheid Movement design
3 1981 Solidarity design produced by the York Community Bookshop
4 Symbol of Soviet Communism
5 Black Rights leader Malcolm X, 1970 design
6 Amnesty International logo produced by 'Creative Promotions' in the 1970s
7 Glittery Karl Marx published by Fly Press 1979
8 Lenin as a child in a plastic star on a metal base
9 Trotsky made by York Community Bookshop
10 Maoist 1970s design
11 Socialist Workers Party design, 1980
12 The Committee of 100 Anti-Vietnam campaign badge of 1967
13 Late 1970s design, publisher unknown
14 and 18 West Country Marketing 1978 designs
15 El Salvador solidarity campaign, 1981
16 Palestine solidarity campaign, 1979
17 Anarchy design by the Tea Pot Club 1980
19 Fly Press design
20 1960s Irish Republican design
21 and 25 Produced by Information on Ireland
22 Troops Out movement design from late 1970s, made up by White and Lambert
23 and 24 Loyalist designs. The Royal Ulster benevolent fund appeal used badges to raise funds.
26 and 27 Plastics bullets designs of 1981; 26 published by Fly Press

Anti-racism and anti-fascism

Apart from anti-apartheid badges and other international designs such as those for American equal rights campaigns, pre-1970 British anti-racist badges are scarce. It was in the mid-1970s with the emergence of the National Front that a huge anti-racist campaign developed stimulated by the Socialist Workers Party in 1977 after the confrontations at Ladywood and Lewisham.

The Anti-Nazi League, as it became known, issued many different designs. Their own 'official' design with the arrow logo was one of the most popular badges in Britain in 1978, selling well over 50,000. A whole series of badges 'against the nazis' was then issued including Civil Servants, Gays, Miners, Hospital Workers, Engineers and many more. The National Front had some badges made, but many manufacturers refused to produce badges for them, and so they are scarce.

Rock against Racism (RAR) began in 1977. It had been prompted by Eric Clapton's outburst against blacks at a concert in Birmingham, and David Bowie's Hitler-ish posturing from the back of an open landau. The badge 'Nazis are no fun' was designed as an advance ticket for a Rock against Racism gig at the Royal College of Arts in 1977. A five-pointed star was then adopted as RAR's logo and it appeared on many badges with many different colours and slogans.

The inner-city riots of 1981 further fuelled the racist debate. Some of the worst areas affected were Brixton, Toxteth and the St Pauls area of Bristol. The 'Amnesty for St Pauls' badge was produced in two tone black and white. Fly Press produced 'Tory Britain—it's a riot' featuring Mrs Thatcher wearing a policeman's helmet.

The ugly side of Welsh nationalism reared its head in 1979 when several holiday cottages were destroyed by arson attacks. The cottages had English owners and a badge 'Strike a light for Wales', featuring an England's Glory matchbox label, was produced by the Badge Shop in London hoping to cash in on a current issue with a humorous design.

The golly debate

The Robertson's golly has been accused of being a racist symbol by some groups, who have demanded that it be abolished. Forty-eight hours before the Queen opened the 1984 Liverpool Garden Festival Robertson's were asked by the left-wing Merseyside County Council to remove all the gollies from their jam garden. Similarly, the Greater London Council threatened to stop the use of Robertson's jams in schools until the golly was removed. When Merseyside County Council denounced the golly, hundreds of its supporters threatened to stop buying Robertson's jam if the company gave way one inch!

In 1985 Greenwich Council's Race Unit produced a report entitled 'I love my golly'. Among the views, for and against, are snippets of golly history. The report says that in Aden in the 1960s the Argyll and Sutherland Highlanders wore a Robertson's golly badge for each Arab they had killed. Another story says that at one time the wearing of golly brooches by young women was a sign of sexual availability. Around 1980 1,000 gollies were produced with white faces for the United States. The irony of the golly debate is that should they be abolished, they will become even more collectable.

Anti-racism and anti-fascism

Campaigns against the extreme right were mounted by various groups from the mid-1970s onwards, including the Anti-Nazi League (*1*, *5*, *7* to *14*) and Rock Against Racism (*3*, *6*, *16*, *17* and *21*).
2 A clever design using the punk dance, the Pogo, by the Socialist Workers Party, 1978
4 Two-tone Amnesty design, following the 1981 riots in Bristol
7 The 'Bestselling badge of 1978'
15 York Community Bookshop 1979 incorporating the Rastafarian colours
18 Design featuring the Home Secretary William Whitelaw and the Special Patrol Group
19 National Front badges almost disappeared after the Anti-Nazi League's success. Badge manufacturers refused to make them
22 Alternative Anti-Nazi League design against John Travolta and discos, both popular in 1978
23 GLC design made up by London Emblem Company

1

2

3

4

5

6

7

8

9

10

11

12

13

14

15

16

17

18

19

20

21

22

23

Sexual politics

The feminist movement

The origins of the feminist movement go back to the beginning of the century and the Suffragettes. Their determined campaign included many badges, some of which were of the button type, now highly prized by collectors. The Museum of London has several examples.

In 1928, women got the same voting rights as men and by 1979 there was a woman Prime Minister. Despite the apparent success of these early campaigns there are more feminist badges today than ever. The feminist fist appears on hundreds of badges, even on glitter designs. This symbol is the 'mirror of venus' with the fist added and dates from around 1971.

The women's liberation movement was initially treated by the media as a big joke when it began in the 1960s, but became one of the most successful of all the pressure groups, fighting discrimination in all spheres of society. The campaign for equal rights resulted in the Equal Opportunities and Sex Discrimination Act of 1975, which made sex discrimination illegal. 'The best man for the job may be a woman' was one slogan. Spare Rib, an influential feminist magazine, issued 'Fight Sexism in Schools' to attack certain reading schemes used in primary schools where boys were shown helping Dad in the garage and girls helping Mum in the kitchen. ERICCA—Equal Rights in Clubs Campaign for Action—is an interesting badge. This campaign was against working men's clubs with 'men only' bars and similar male-orientated rules.

Other badges strike a more philisophical note: 'It begins when you sink in his arms and end with your arms in his sink' (this slogan has been used by several firms, including West Country Marketing and the York Community Bookshop). 'When God made man she was only experimenting' and 'A woman without a man is like a fish without a bicycle', as well as badges featuring 'Mother' Christmas, were made in vast numbers.

Other campaigns for women include those against male violence by the National Women's Aid Federation, and the National Abortion Campaign against the Corrie Bill of 1979, which they feared would lead to a return to back-street abortions.

Gay rights

The fight for gay rights developed alongside the feminist movement. Gay News issued a badge featuring moral campaigner Mary Whitehouse stating 'Gay News fights on'. In 1977 Gay News had published a poem about a Roman centurian's homosexual thoughts as he lifted Christ from the Cross. Mrs Whitehouse brought a private prosecution for blasphemy—the first for 56 years. The Love That Dares to Speak its Name, by James Kirkup was found to contain 'the most scurrilous profanity'. Gay News was fined £1,000 and the editor was given a nine months' suspended sentence. In 1977 'Lesbians Ignite' is a badge that got a Miss Boychuk the sack. Her boss, who worked for a stockbroker, said that the badge would make him the laughing stock of the Arab world and an industrial tribunal agreed. Other gay badges have provoked strong responses from moral campaigners, 'I don't give a f . . .—a woman's right to choose' and 'I'm a f . . . . . . queer' among them.

Many modern feminist badges feature the fist symbol of the Women's Liberation Movement, a design dating from about 1971 (*1*, *2*, *10*, *12*, *19* and *24*).
2 Glitter badge by Fly Press
3 Women together from Gay Liberation Front Information Service
4, 8, 9, 11, 14 and 25 Designs by York Community Bookshop
5, 6 and 20 Designs from Spare Rib
7 National Union of Students
12, 16 and 26 National Abortion Campaign
13 1981 Fly Press design
17 Gay News design
19 National Women's Aid Federation
21 and 22 Gay Liberation Front Information Service

Campaigns against the cuts

Unemployment

The Socialist Worker's Party was the main organization behind the 'Right to Work' march to Blackpool in 1977. The next eight years saw a steady rise in unemployment figures. People marched for jobs and badges were struck to commemorate their efforts. One such march was the 'Back to Jarrow' march in November 1981, recalling the first Jarrow march in the 1930s.

The parallel with the 1930s continued when, in 1982, the government minister Norman Tebbit said his father had looked for work by cycling until he found it. Cries of 'On your bike, Tebbit' followed and a badge showing a bike and the phrase 'I can do that gis a job' was published. The slogan came from Alan Bleasdale's *Boys from the Blackstuff*, a television drama featuring an unemployed Liverpudlian, Yosser Hughes. The humour continued to shine through the adversity with badges such as 'Unemployment isn't working'. 'Jobs not Yops' was a reaction to the hopelessness of the Youth Opportunities Scheme, which had replaced earlier job creation programmes and was seen by many as a way for employers to get cheap labour.

Cuts in services

In 1979 Margaret Thatcher became Prime Minister on a platform of tax cuts. To raise the money, she attacked the public sector with vigour. Her public service cuts led to a large wave of protest and badges, initially in 1979–80, and then later in 1983–85, when the Labour councils fought the government's attempt to impose a 'legal' rate. Many local boroughs issued badges, spending rates to do so!

The fightback campaign issued a series of badges through 1980, many featuring a powerful symbol of two hands breaking an axe and the names of different boroughs. 'Push for more Nurseries' is a delightful design (by the York Community Bookshop), as is the 'Birmingham children's defence campaign—stop the chop'. 'Save London Transport' written on the London Transport logo was used during the 'Fares fair' campaign. The GLC followed South Yorkshire's lead and lowered fares to encourage more people to use public transport, but the government overruled their decision. The *Morning Star* issued 25,000 of the badges and then the GLC continued to issue this very popular design. The debate continued and a 'Save our Buses—Bus campaign' was put out in 1984.

Other councils such as Leicester, Merseyside and South Yorkshire were also being forced to cut their spending drastically. South Yorkshire launched 'CAT the campaign against takeover'. In Leicester the council led a campaign to promote its bus services 'Your Leicester City Bus serving Leicester serving You'. As well as the $1\frac{1}{2}$ in (38 mm) button badge they issued plastic clip-on badges in different languages for the city's immigrant population.

Cuts in the National Health Service affected many hospitals. NUPE issued 'I love the NHS' with a heart substituted for the word love. This design originated from 'I love (Heart) NY' a popular slogan in the United States. The Loughborough hospital was one of many affected and a 'Save our Hospital' campaign raged in 1984. Similarly, in 1982, a decision was made to close the Tadworth Court Children's Hospital.

Fight-back campaigns

From 1977 to 1985 a variety of groups published badges supporting campaigns for the right to work and against government cuts.
2 and **8** Labour Party designs. **8** is a Westfield moulded plastic badge
4 and **7** Rank and File design
6 and **13** York Community Bookshop badges
10 The *Sun* 19 November 1982 launched a media campaign to save Tadworth Children's hospital
11 and **19** Badges from NUPE
17 and **18** Leicester City Council. *18* is a 1984 plastic design and reads 'Your city council working for you'. For the benefit of the Asian community it was to be found in five languages: Hindi, Punjabi, Gujarati, Bengali, and Urdu as well as English
20 Fightback campaign
22 and 23 'Keep GLC working for London' was the slogan in 1984 as the GLC faced extinction at the hands of the government. 'Save it' appears on many designs. Some pro-government designs also appeared, such as 'You'll be better off without the GLC'.
24 Open University Students Association

48

Pacifism

In 1934 Canon Dick Shepherd wrote to newspapers asking for those who opposed war to write to him with the pledge 'I renounce war and will never support or sanction another.' Tens of thousands replied and as a result of this response he formed the Peace Pledge Union. An enamel badge with the letters PPU was adopted, but it would have taken a brave person to wear it from 1939–45. Since the war, and especially since the 1960s, PPU has issued many button designs.

In 1958 the first Aldermaston march took place, organized by the Campaign for Nuclear Disarmament (CND). Shortly before, Gerald Holton had designed the now famous symbol. According to Holton, the design can be explained in two ways: first, it is the semaphore signal for ND, nuclear disarmament, and, secondly, the broken cross means the death of mankind with the circle representing the unborn child. This powerful symbol has appeared on millions of badges worldwide, and become instantly recognizable.

Eric Austin of Kensington first made the design into a badge. It was no ordinary badge, but made of pottery to survive the holocaust. Since then badges have been struck in silver, enamel and plastic, but the vast majority are button badges. Many designs of Aldermaston Easter marches include the date, which is useful for collectors.

The emphasis of the peace campaign has varied according to the state of the arsenals of the world's leading powers. In the early 1970s, Polaris 'The deadly white elephant' was the target, with 'Scrap Polaris'. In the early 1980s Cruise missiles were arriving in Europe from the United States and a women's protest centred on Greenham Common where the first missiles were to be deployed. CND launched a massive national campaign. Many local CND groups produced badges for sale at local and national peace rallies. For one of the larger 1980 rallies, the 'Protest and survive' badge was designed, depicting a Cruise missile broken by the CND symbol. Many designs were aimed at President Reagan and Margaret Thatcher. 'Send Thatcher on a Cruise' was a big seller. A whole series of 'against the bomb' badges were made, from 'Families against the bomb' to a badge featuring Noddy which reads 'Toytown Young Conservatives against Cruise and Trident'. At least 30 different variations on this theme are known, and there will probably be more.

Wearing a particular badge can generate a strong response. In April 1985 Devon Education Authority banned teachers from wearing CND badges. There was no real evidence of CND activity or indoctrination, but Conservative Council leader Ted Pinney said, 'The aim is to remove politics from the classroom.' Harry Brokenshaw, Devon's NUT secretary described the decision as 'bigotry gone mad'. Vicky Rollason asked the NUT conference on 10 April 1985, 'May I wear a union badge or a car sticker? May I carry a copy of the *Daily Mirror*, or even, Heaven forbid, the *Sun*?'

Like all popular slogans or symbols, humorous alternatives have been produced. The 'Y Fronts Prevent Fallout' badge using the CND symbol for the Y was current at the peak of Cruise, 1981–82. Their common theme and symbol makes CND badges most collectable. In a Christian CND protest outside the Ministry of Defence on 27 May 1985 The Rev Ayred Willets was festooned with over 100 CND badges.

Peace

Most pacifist badges from 1960 to 1985 have been published by CND, locally and nationally.
11, 12, 18 to **20**, and **23** to **29** 1980s designs, many against Cruise and Trident.
17 and **21** Peace Pledge Union designs
24 A homemade design, one of many varieties of 'Against the bomb' badges produced since 1980
29 SANE is Students against Nuclear Energy
30 A rare attempt at a nuclear joke

The ecology movement

The environmental movement and its badges owe much to the influential pressure group Friends of the Earth. In May 1971, when Friends of the Earth was formed, they returned millions of non-returnable bottles to Schweppes, an amusing stunt that brought home a serious message. By 1985 there were bottle banks all over Britain. A more serious matter than bottles however, was the energy debate.

Energy

The 'Nuclear Power—No thanks' Smiling Sun was created in April 1975 by an anti-nuclear group in Arhus, Denmark. From late 1976 the Smiling Sun became a symbol of international solidarity in the anti-nuclear movement. The design became known worldwide, just as the CND symbol had done. The badge appeared in over 30 languages, all of them obtainable in Britain, although the more obscure ones were hard to find. The copyright to the Smiling Sun was given to the *Organisationen til Oplysning om Atomkraft* with the specification that all profits should be used for activities and information to bring about a non-nuclear world. OOA were quick to trademark the symbol to protect it from commercial use, but it is unlikely that the profits from a humorous 'bootleg' of 1981 'Ageing hippies no thanks' were used to bring about a non-nuclear world!

Friends of the Earth were one of the UK distributors of the Smiling Sun. They also produced several of their own designs. 'Windscale it'll cost the Earth' was distributed in 1977 after the public enquiry closed in November. The leak in a nuclear reactor at Three Mile Island in Pennsylvania in 1979 heightened the nuclear debate. The Energy Council struck back with a set of badges: 'Atoms for Energy', 'Dark Age no thanks', 'Stone Age no thanks', and 'Ice Age no thanks'.

Alongside the anti-nuclear lobby ran alternative energy campaigns—for solar, wind and water power. One badge embraced all three—'Energy Sun Wind and Water'—part of a set of over 50 ecology badges produced by Tantra designs. The oil crisis of the mid-1970s ensured the success devoted to saving energy.

Pollution

Friends of the Earth also campaigned for re-cycling. 'I'm a paper saver' was was a sister badge to 'Plant a Tree', of which there are many varieties. Anti-pollution campaigns have given rise to great public interest as well as numerous badges, including 'Bio-degradable plastic now', and 'Lead-free petrol now' (both Tantra designs).

An official anti-pollution campaign was concerned with keeping the streets litter-free. The Keep Britain Tidy logo became commonplace in the early 1970s and has been used by many local litter campaigns. The City of Glasgow's Department of Cleansing issued a set of six badges to that effect in the late 1970s, along with another design featuring 'Captain Clean'. The Wombles were pressed into service during the peak of their popularity in 1975: 'I'm a Womble—I keep Britain tidy' was issued (London Emblem Company). Walt Disney characters were also used in the late 1970s. Humourous counterparts include 'Clean up the City, eat a pigeon'. In the early 1980s the Keep Britain Tidy group initiated an 'I'm backing a Beautiful Britain' campaign for which several badges were produced.

Energy and pollution were two concerns of the ecology movement. 'Keep Britain Tidy' was a more official campaign.
1 to **5** The Smiling Sun, created in 1975, was translated into well over 30 languages, as well as being used on the bootleg (5)
6 One of the set of 'Atoms for Energy' issued by the Energy Council around 1980
7 Karen Silkwood died in suspicious circumstances in a car accident whilst pursuing allegations over safety practices at a uranium processing plant in 1974. She became a martyr for the movement and this badge was produced by Better Badges.
8, 10, 13, and **15** Tantra designs. *13* is from a set, and the others are from well over 50 ecological designs of the late 1970s
9 and **11** Friends of the Earth designs 1977. *9* was produced for the Windscale enquiry of 1977. Windscale later became known as Sellafield
12 Sunflower logo of Ecology Party, 1982. The Ecology Party became the Green Party in 1985
14 Friends of the Earth design made up by White and Lambert
16 to **23** Keep Tidy designs, 1975 to 1984. *20* is part of a set using Disney characters

Conservation

Since 1945, the effects of pollution and the destruction of animal habitats worldwide, has meant a rapid growth in the number of organizations concerned with the protection of species and their environment.

From its inception in 1961 until 1978 the World Wildlife Fund spent £15,000,000 on approximately 1,900 projects in 135 countries, some of the money having been raised through selling badges. The world-famous Panda symbol was designed by Sir Peter Scott, the naturalist. It has appeared on countless badges. In 1981 to mark the twentieth anniversary of WWF, Operation Survival was mounted in conjunction with Golden Wonder (manufacturers of crisps). For every 10 tokens from Golden Wonder packets a free badge was given and 10p was donated to the fund by Golden Wonder. It was hoped to raise £45,000—meaning they intended to give away 450,000 badges! There were 10 different designs: zebra, gorilla, elephant, cheetah, rhino, falcon, Operation Survival symbol, land rover, helicopter and a World Wildlife Fund twentieth-year badge. They were manufactured by the London Emblem Company.

In the mid-1970s two similar sets were issued. 'I'm helping the animals' was a set of eight badges issued in conjunction with Smith's crisps: gorilla, hippopotamus, rhino, lion, tiger, elephant, polar bear, and panda. They were issued as lithographs and acetates. 'Save the Whale' with Matey (Bubble Bath) and the World Wildlife Fund was a set of six badges each showing different whales.

Between 1981 and 1982 the World Wildlife Fund got together with Rainbow Designs (London Emblem Company) and produced a whole series of badges entitled 'Threatened Species Series'. These 2⅛ in (55 mm) designs were initially issued on cards onto which the badge was pinned along with information about the particular threatened species. Later they were sold separately in two sizes. Further designs were added with the slogan 'Survival—we're in it together'.

Along similar lines Marjorie Bromley designed a set of badges with the theme 'I'm for Wildlife'. These were sold through the Royal Society for Nature Conservation. In 1981 the set consisted of 12 designs: blue butterfly, puffin, hedgehog, badger, wren, deer fawn, frog, grey seal pup, otter, owl, squirrel, and rabbit. Since then, the set has grown and the slogans 'I love butterflies', 'I'm for birds' and 'I'm for wildflowers' have been adopted.

RSPB's Young Ornithologists Club issued a set of four 'Save the birds' badges in 1978, and about 1983, a set of six woodland birds: willowtit, wood warbler, jay, chaffinch, wren and spotted flycatcher. An early 1970s set of 'Save the birds' also exists, mainly lithographs.

Smith's Crisps were once again involved in 1978, when the PDSA used them to support the 'I'm helping the pets' campaign. There were eight badges in the set: rabbit, dog, guinea pig, budgie, tortoise, hamster, cat and parrot. The RSPCA issued a set of five 'Pets Care' badges in 1984, featuring 'Henry's Cat'; 'Don't give pets as gifts', 'Pets care counts', 'Don't forget to exercise your dog', 'Meet my pig she's my friend' and 'Some of my best friends are animals'.

Many metal or enamel designs have been issued on behalf of animal trusts, groups, and clubs.

Conservation

Animals are always popular on badges, especially in support of a good cause.

1 to 4 The World Wildlife Panda designed by Sir Peter Scott appears on many badges. *1* is a plastic badge. *2* is part of the Operation Survival set (*23*), a campaign sponsored by Golden Wonder Crisps. *3* is the original Panda Club design of 1961 made up by Gaunt of Birmingham for 5- to 10-year-olds

5 World Wildlife Fund. A Wildlife Ranger's enamel (made by Marples and Beasley) for 11- to 18-year-olds

6, 9, 10, and 21 RSPCA designs. 6 is by Marples and Beasley. 9 One of a set of five 1984 designs using Henry's Cat. 21 Design current in 1950s and 1960s

7 One of a set that grew and grew in the early 1980s, designed by Marjorie Bramley for the Royal Society for Nature Conservation

8, 22 to 25 Sponsorship by large companies is popular in this category

11, 16 and 18 Examples of local groups badges. *11* is by White and Lambert

12 One of a set of four RSPB Young Ornithologists Club designs, 1978

13 One of a set of six 1982 RSPB designs

14 One of a set of RSPB lithographs of the early 1970s

15 One of Rainbow Designs' 'Threatened Species' series originally issued in 2⅛ in (55 mm), re-issued in 1983 in 1½ in (38 mm)

17 1985 Forestry Commission design

19 People's Dispensary for Sick Animals Juniors Club—The Busy Bees

20 Young People's Trust for Endangered Species, 1982 White and Lambert

Animal welfare

Judging by the numbers of badges on the subject, Britain is indeed a nation of animal lovers. Animal welfare was initially the concern of charities like the RSPCA and PDSA but has now entered the political arena. It is not true to say that the anti-bloodsports lobby only began to obtain media attention in the 1970s and 1980s, as the League Against Cruel Sports was founded in 1924, and the National Anti-Vivisection Society in 1875. However, bloodsports, animal experiments, vivisection and the plight of whales in particular, have all been animal campaigns that through the 1970s became more political in outlook. Pressure groups led protests against fishing, hare coursing, and in particular, fox hunting. 'For fox sake ban hunting' is a well-used slogan on badges. 'Only rotters hunt otters' was a badge that won the day when hunting otters was finally made illegal in 1977. 'Don't badger the badger' is a well-designed badge by Friends of the Earth. The Field Sports Association produced a set of 'Field sports supporter' badges showing a fish, a pheasant and a horse, amongst others.

Save the whale

Greenpeace began in 1971 out of a protest about a bomb test in Alaska. Their success saw the organization grow internationally. They were one of the first environmental groups that believed in direct action, although not damage to property, and their excursions in *Rainbow Warrior* did much to protect whales and seals. Many firms produced badges to support their campaign. In the United States a set of oval button badges featuring whales had sold in huge quantities and some of these found their way to Britain. West Country Marketing adopted the government's 'Save it' energy campaign slogan and stamped it on a sperm whale. Friends of the Earth and Tantra designs, among others, also produced whale badges.

Save the seal

'Save the Seal' was another very sensitive issue which, at the time of the annual culls, created much media attention. Greenpeace was once again at the heart of the action, supported by many animal-loving groups, several of whom produced badges. 'Save my skin save my life' was an RSPCA design, 'Fur coats—wear fake' was by Tantra, and 'Save our Seals' by the Animal Welfare Trust.

Anti-vivisection

In June 1979 a magazine called *The Beast* was published, dealing with issues such as the beagles used in smoking experiments. This magazine was founded without capital and grew from the sales of a single badge.

In 1979 and 1980 Better Badges produced a set of animal liberation badges. Most of these designs featured endangered species, but one had a chicken's head on it. This indicated the beginning of a shift in emphasis towards campaigns against animal experiments. The British Union for the Abolition of Vivisection produced 'I'm cut up about vivisection'. Further designs followed as the campaign gathered momentum. Attacks on laboratories, such as Porton Down, by the Animal Liberation Front followed, and beagles and mink were set free.

Animal campaigns include anti-bloodsports, anti-vivisection and anti-factory farming.

1 and **2** Part of a set of 13 published by *The Beast* and made by Better Badge, 1979–80

3, 4, 6, 9 and **21** Examples of well over 50 ecological badges produced by Tantra Designs in the late 1970s to early 1980s

5 and **18** Hunt Saboteurs Association of 1979 (5) compared with late 1930s leatherette Hunt Supporters Association badge made by W J Mogridge of Bristol

7 The Humane Research Trust began in 1974, and this is their principal badge, supplied by Hannah. Like many other such groups they have their own machine and produce small runs and single designs

8, 10, and **19** British Union for the Abolition of Vivisection designs of the early 1980s

11 and **13** to **15** Clever anti-bloodsports designs of the early 1980s. *11* is by the Young Liberals

12 and **17** Many badges were sold to raise funds for Greenpeace, the group whose daring activities to save whales and seals gained them much publicity and support from the late 1970s onwards

16 One of a set of at least five 'Field Sports Supporter' designs issued since 1979

20 West Country Marketing supplied this badge which incorporates the energy campaign logo of the mid-1970s, 'Save it', stamped onto a sperm whale

22 Friends of the Earth whale design of the early 1980s

Clubs and societies

The boom in the enamel badge business in the 1880s was in part due to the rise of sporting clubs, trade unions and a variety of other groups. Children's clubs were also in their early stages; these include the Boys Brigade (1883), Church Lads Brigade (1891), Girls Life Brigade (1901), Boy Scouts (1907) and Girl Guides (1910).

This section looks in particular at religious, charitable, transport, sporting and school- or youth-based groups. Many of the other types of clubs that have developed since 1945 are to be found in other sections of this book.

Many youth organizations, such as the Scouts have issued promotional badges as well as their sew-on and metal uniform badges. (A club has been in existence since 1956 for collectors of such badges.) In 1957 the centenary of Baden-Powell was greeted with a 1 in (25 mm) button badge in black and white. Baden-Powell is also on a 1¼ in (32 mm) design produced for Baden-Powell House in the 1970s. In the 1980s the Scouts produced a set of button badges, including 'Scouts are magic', 'Scouts worldwide' and 'Cubs are great'. Other Scouting badges include those for anniversaries, gang shows, 'Cub Scout tea challenge' and various camps and jamborees. Other similar organizations to issue promotional badges include the Boys Brigade, Girls Brigade and various youth clubs.

The eternal popularity of collecting stamps can be seen by the number of Stamp Bugs around. The button badge 'I'm a stamp bug', produced in 1980 for a national campaign in schools, is relatively common. One variation shows the 'Stamp Bug' complete with Union Jack trousers, and 'I'm a stamp bug' in blue above.

A variety of stamp clubs flourished in the 1960s all with their own badges such as Ace Stamp Club, (the badge features the Cape of Good Hope triangular stamp), Universal Stamp Club and Philatelic Services Stamp Club (both designs feature the globe). Many local stamp clubs also have badges made. Similarly, many numismatic clubs (coin collectors) exist and they have badges, often metal or enamel. Other groups, such as bottle collectors and even badge collectors, have badges. The Badge Collectors Circle was founded in 1980 and their first design was produced by Tantra. Later badges were 'homemade', until in 1985 The Universal Button Company produced their 'I'm a 1985 Badger'.

It is interesting when some of the more obscure groups of the past turn up and claim our attention in the form of a badge. The 'Rose Hip Collectors Club' for example, produced several year badges in the 1960s. Scientific, historical, and geographical societies are all badge wearers. The York Archeological Trust and similar groups sell badges to raise funds for their digs. Societies such as 'Robin Hood Society' or the 'Roundhead Association' sell badges to raise money for costumes. Various horticultural societies produce badges, whether they be locally run or national groups such as the Royal Horticultural Society. Organizations for dog lovers, old people, horse riders, magicians and even the Interplanetary Space Travel Research Group (UK) have at least one thing in common—they all produce badges.

Clubs and societies

The badge is the mark of membership of a wide range of clubs and societies.

1 and **2** Scouting movement button badges. *1* is a 1957 commemorative featuring Baden-Powell, *2* a Silver Jubilee camp design

3 and **4** Two 1950s to 1960s stamp club designs. *3* is a White and Lambert

5 Gaunt of Birmingham made this 1963 Rose Hip Collectors Club badge

6 Majorettes design of late 1970s made by White and Lambert

7 and **18** The National Trust, founded in 1895, owns over 230 historic houses, nearly 450,000 acres of our finest countryside and 400 miles of unspoilt coastline. Both badges are from the 1970s

8, **28**, and **30** Other youth group badges of the 1970s

10 The Badge Collectors Circle was founded in 1980. Original Badge was made by Tantra designs

11 In 1985 the Badge Collectors Circle had this excellent design made by the Universal Button Company

12 Robin Hood Society, a Westfield moulded plastic badge

13 1930s Thomas Fattorini Ltd button badge for a touring association

14 and **15** The Friendly Society and the International Order of Oddfellows ornate designs, similar in many ways to early trade union badges. *14* is a mirror back, and *15* an early button badge of 1910

16 1920s enamel of the Women's League of Health and Beauty founded by Prunella Stack. Badge by Vaughtons of Birmingham

9, **17**, and **19** to **26** Mixed bag of other clubs, societies and associations. *22* is the International Brotherhood of Magicians. *24* is the Cocker Spaniel Club. *25* Evergreen Clubs are for pensioners

27 Stamp Bug 1980 standard design; there is also a 'Bitten by the stamp bug' version

Officers' badges

A vast range of enamel and button badges exists for school 'officers' and club officials. School badges are commoner than the others. These disappeared gradually through the 1970s and 1980s, but remained in many grammar and public schools, usually in enamel.

Schools

In 1936 the Universal Button Company carried $\frac{7}{8}$ in (22 mm) and 1 in (25 mm) button badges in red, blue, green and yellow with the following 24 titles: Captain, Vice-Captain, School Captain, Form Captain, House Captain, Class Captain, Room Captain, Team Captain, House Vice-Captain, Sports, Craftsman, Swimming, Leader, Prefect, Monitor, Monitress, Merit, Conduct, House Prefect, Vice-Prefect, Head Boy, Head Girl, Boys Club, Girls Club. Other companies offered similar designs and many variations exist. The name of the school was sometimes written in the bar—Chester Road Girls of Port Sunlight is an example dating from the 1920s. Later varieties include the treble clef sign for music, or the pen nib for handwriting. Merit badges in the form of stars also exist. Plain colour badges are also common and are found in $1\frac{1}{4}$ in (32 mm) as well as $\frac{7}{8}$ in (22 mm) and 1 in (25 mm) varieties. The following colours have all been used: red, blue, green, white, orange, pale blue, royal blue, pink, brown, purple and black.

At least since the 1920s many companies have issued schools enamels as stock designs. Two companies have dominated this market, Fattorini and Sons Ltd and Thomas Fattorini Ltd. In 1983 Thomas Fattorini Ltd finally took control of Fattorini and Sons Ltd, and their catalogue of that year showed the vast range of enamels available— well over 100 designs in four different colours. These included shields and bars in a variety of shapes and a total of 36 different sports and activities badges, including computers. *Swyddog* is an interesting addition, being Welsh for 'prefect'.

Other officials

Badge manufacturers have also held stocks of similarly designed buttons and enamels for the officials of clubs and societies. These are not as common as school badges but some examples do turn up, especially 'Steward' and 'President'. In 1936 the Universal Button Company offered at least 36 button badge designs in black and white $\frac{7}{8}$ in (22 mm) (at ninepence per dozen or nine shillings per gross) and further ranges in blue and white $1\frac{1}{4}$ in (32 mm) (at one shilling and sixpence per dozen). These include the following titles: Committee, Secretary, Hon Sec, Asst Sec, Treasurer, Executive Committee, Starter, Judge, Umpire, Referee, Lapscorer, Handicapper, Delegate, Trustee, Council, Visitor, Stallholder, Doorkeeper, M C, Whip, Clerk of the Course, Demonstrator, Marshall and many others. They were also offering enamels in a variety of designs, at prices ranging from six shillings and ninepence per dozen for a plain design, to eleven shillings and threepence per dozen for a more ornate badge.

Officials' badges for conferences, exhibitions or fairs have been made in ornate enamel, plastic or even card and leatherette. Some of these simply show the delegate's status or rank; others include the company or society's name. Through the 1970s the trend was towards plastic badges such as Thomas Fattorini's 'Universal personal badges'.

Officers

A badge is also a useful way of proclaiming the status of its wearer.
1 to **14** School officers button badges. *1* is a 1920s badge worn by Sheila McCaig when she went to Chester Rd Girls Schools in Port Sunlight. *6* is one of at least eight plain colours. *7* is for music; *11* for merit; *12* for handwriting; *13* for reading
15 to **24** School officers enamelled badges mostly made by Thomas Fattorini Ltd or Fattorini and Sons. *19* Swyddog is 'prefect' in Welsh
25 Adult officers enamel badge
26 to **32** Adult officers button badges
33 and **34** Card and leatherette officers badges
35 Child's sheriff badge
37 Thomas Fattorini Ltd enamel issued to workers of Herbert Morris Ltd, Loughborough
38 Exhibitor's badge produced by Sir D G Collins
39 Conference enamel badge for the International Solvent Extraction Conference
40 Royal Horticultural Society long-service badge, issued to Jack Haley, a Kentish man who worked for over 40 years as a gardener in Ypres, Belgium for the Commonwealth War Graves Commission
41 1980s Thomas Fattorini Ltd plastic staff badge

Safety

Road

The Royal Society for the Prevention of Accidents orginated in 1916 as the London Safety First Association, later becoming the National Safety First Association before becoming ROSPA. The red triangle of safety was adopted before the Second World War and has appeared on many badges of local safety societies and associations, and also during national campaigns. Who remembers learning their kerb drill in 1960? 'Look right, look left, look right again, if all's clear then cross'. If you were able to perform this properly you got your kerb drill badge courtesy of Walls Ice Cream. Not to be left out, Mr Whippy issued their safety club badge and 'Mr Softee says safety first' was used on at least two designs. Lyons Maid, too, had a badge: 'Mind how you go'. Also in the 1960s, Esso Petrol awarded road safety badges. These were plastic and issued by Coco the Clown himself.

As well as the kerb drill, ROSPA initiated the Tufty Club. Since its beginnings in 1961 it has issued a standard badge featuring Tufty that comes in a variety of fittings. Probably because the badge was to be worn by the very young it was normally issued with a safety pin fitting (with at least two types of solid back), but a normal fixing was also available. The design has been reissued many times as have badges featuring the slogan 'Stop, look and listen before crossing the road' printed on a design in a variety of loud colours. By 1985 the Tufty Club had 24,500 members.

In the early 1970s the Department of Transport initiated the Green Cross Code. This was well publicized in a massive TV campaign, and accompanying badges. In the mid-1970s the Green Cross Man was first used. The standard badge featured the Green Cross Man and the slogan 'Always use the Green Cross Code—take it from Green Cross Man'. At least four other standard designs are known, along with many local designs such as 'I'm a Suffolk Cross Coder'. The Green Cross Man was still being issued in 1985.

Other safety campaigns

National cycling proficiency was introduced in 1958 by ROSPA and a standard enamel badge featuring the red triangle was adopted. Pinches and J R Gaunt were among the main manufacturers. ROSPA also have training schemes, with badges, for motorcyclists and even for fork-lift truck drivers.

Other children's safety campaigns include 'Stay off the line and stay alive', a late 1970s railway safety campaign. One of two known designs features Mr Silly of Mr Men fame. Other railway designs include 'I don't play on the railway' and 'Play safe stay safe'.

The Royal Life Saving Society has issued several designs for water safety, including enamels. 'I'm into water safety with Valerie Vole' was another large campaign of the 1980s. 'The Sun says belt up' was a badge specially produced to help promote the new laws regarding seat belts in early 1983. 'Don't drink and drive' campaign badges are not common but do exist.

In 1979 the police force celebrated 150 years of service, and invited children to be an 'Eye of the Law'. Similar police campaigns have produced many badges, such as 'Crimestop Lanarkshire '68'.

Issuing a badge helps to make a safety campaign popular with children.

1 to **7**, **19**, **20** and **25** The red triangle was adopted by the National Safety First Association which started in 1916 and later became ROSPA—Europe's largest safety organization dealing with accident prevention. *1* and *2* are 1950s; *3* 1960s enamel; *4* 1931 enamel by Denton and Down, London; *6* is by John Pinches, London 1968; *19* and *20* ice cream safety designs include the kerb drill (as does *22*). *25* is the ROSPA 'glow worm' reflective badge of 1980

8 to **13** Road safety designs. *10* is an early 1960s design for the Tufty Club. *11* is a 1970s design made up by White and Lambert with a safety-pin attachment. *12* is also a White and Lambert crimp. *13* is a plastic badge of the 1960s issued by a stalwart safety promoter, Coco the Clown

14 to **18** Green Cross Code designs. *15* to *17* are early 1970s designs, White and Lambert crimps. *14* is a later 1970s design, when the Green Cross man was adopted. *18* is a 'glow rim' badge by Westfield Advertising in conjunction with Rix petrol

23 A reminder by the *Sun* in March 1983 of the new seat belt law which has since saved many lives

24 Mr Silly was used in 1978 to keep children off railway lines

26 A second-surface printed insert into a stamped metal back for the RLSS around 1980

27 A White and Lambert crimp used to promote the 150th anniversary of the police force in 1979

28 and **29** Two look-out badges—one for crime and one for pedestrians around 1978

Health

Encouraging children to clean their teeth has not always been easy and many designs of badge exist to help in this task, some produced by the British Health Foundation and some by toothpaste manufacturers. Crest toothpaste's design of 1982 'The band of busy brushers, an elephant never forgets do you?' was very popular, along with 'Keep your smile like the crocodile'.

The 'Sport for all' campaign of 1977 produced at least two designs featuring the logo, and the 1979 'Look after yourself' campaign produced a badge with the logo issued in 1½ in (38 mm) and 2⅛ in (55 mm) sizes.

'No smoking' was one of the bigger health issues in the 1960s and 1970s. In 1982 a campaign featuring the evil 'Nick o Teen' was directed at youngsters and two badges were produced. In 1980 Better Badges produced 'Submerge the urge' featuring a sinking cigarette. There were at least two designs of this. At this time smoking in public was under scrutiny. The Socialist Medical Association's slogan 'You smoke we choke' was put on a badge, and when it became unlawful to smoke in various public places in the early 1980s London Transport issued a badge with 'No smoking' in the centre of their famous symbol.

Other school badges

The Pre-school Playgroups Association was founded in 1961, and they have a standard design featuring their logo. They have also published designs for such occasions as the 1977 Silver Jubilee, and International Year of the Child.

Various play schemes have used badges since the mid-1970s. The majority of these are button badges. The Barrow-upon-Soar Community Association Playgroup Scheme (BOSCAPS) produced their first button badge in 1977. In 1981 they decided to change to a plastic moulded badge. Westfield was the supplier of both button and the plastic badge, but the button badge had been made up by White and Lambert.

In the days when most schools had a uniform, the school badge was normally embroidered on the blazer pocket. Many schools also had enamel and button badges carrying the school name, motto and emblem. These are still being produced but are not common.

Other school badges worthy of mention are those of STS, the Schools Travel Service. Many thousands of these badges—a simple 'STS' in black on a two-coloured background—have been made.

Schools are an obvious starting point for many publicity campaigns directed at the young. The 'Fanfare for Young Musicians' competition organized through schools has an annual badge featuring the date and logo.

Health

1 One of two 1982 campaign badges from the Health Education Council
2 Better Badges, 1980
3 to 5, 12 and 13 Other health campaigns. 5 is from the 1980 campaign and was made in vast quantities. *12* and *13* are from the 1977 Sport for All campaign
6 to 11 Teeth campaigns 1950s to 1980s. 7 to 9 are made up by White and Lambert. *10* and *11* are from a 1981 campaign which involved Crest toothpaste
14 to 27 School and pre-school button badges. 'I hate skool' has been produced in many guises since the 1960s
16 and 17 STS is the Schools Travel Service (late 1960s design)
19 The Pre-school Playgroups Association began in 1961; this badge is from the early 1970s
20 1979 design
21 and 22 BOSCAPS, the Barrow-upon-Soar Community Association Playgroup Scheme, used a button badge in 1977, but by 1981 it was replaced by a Westfield moulded plastic paint-filled badge
25 and 26 Fanfare for the Young Musicians is a televized competition for school musicians
27 Many schools issue their own badge, often a button badge. This is a White and Lambert badge

Charities

By 1985 there were well over 140,000 registered charities and most of them issue badges of one sort or another. Many date from 1960 when the Charities Register began. The Charities Digest, published annually, provides an excellent guide for the badge collector.

Badges have been used for promotion and fund-raising since many of the charities began. From the turn of the century to 1945 many types of charity badge were devoted to raising funds for hospitals, as hospitals used to rely on charity for their upkeep. A whole host of pageants and carnivals were held, often annually, to raise money. Often the word 'Immune' or 'Immunity' was used on the badge to show that the bearer had paid. Badges were also worn to show that a person was an official 'Collector'.

Rag weeks

One group of the community who have always, it seems, done a lot of good charity work are students. Rag week, the combination of raising money and having a good time, is a popular charity event in colleges and universities. Many Rag week organizers have adopted a logo of some sort which reappears annually. Sheffield students have 'Twikker' and in 1980 celebrated '50 years of Twikker'. 'Funny Ferdy Frog' appears in Bradford, and in Manchester a matchstick man hitting himself on the head often appears. A variety of 'Immune' badges appear for Rag weeks also, and some students, such as those in Stafford, are more direct with their 'I hate students' badge. Sometimes student charity develops out of other activities. In Ripon College the success of 'Colditz', a newsletter devoted to the 'prisoners 1975–77' within the college, resulted in various fund-raising activities including a revue and badge.

Appeal funds

Many charity appeals are for a specific purpose rather than a general fund. Raising money for a minibus or for a hospital extension are two examples. In 1984 the *Sun* newspaper appealed for people to send in ½p coins. The ½p coin was to be withdrawn from circulation in March 1985, and the *Sun*'s 'Give a tiddler, save a toddler' badge helped raise £1,500,000 by March 1985. By this time the appeal had become 'The Ben Hardwick Fund'. Ben Hardwick, a two-year-old, had featured on the television programme *That's Life* in 1984, to publicize the fact that he, and other children, were dying for need of organ transplants. Ben Hardwick got his transplant, but eventually died in 1985.

In 1979 it was the International Year of the Child, and a variety of badges featuring the logo were issued by many charitable concerns. Gunnar Nilsson was a famous Formula One grand prix driver struck down by a fatal illness. The appeal fund, including a badge, raised enough money to open a Gunnar Nilsson ward in a hospital.

In 1981 the Giving for a Living campaign, launched to raise £1,000,000 for research into child medicine, included a badge.

Charities

The badge is a good fund-raiser. **1** to **5** 1930s designs for carnivals and pageants. *3* is by Thomas Fattorini Ltd. *5* is a Fattorini and Sons enamel
6 to **21** Student charity rag badges from 1968 to 1985. *6, 8* and *13* are from Manchester University. *9* was made by Universal Button Company in a lot of 600. *12* follows up the idea of the 1977 Ian Dury badges. *16* is a design for North Yorkshire Area and was made by West Country Marketing. *20* was one of many 1985 appeals for Africa, spin-offs of 'Live Aid'

Charity and the media

The use of well-known personalities to raise money for various charities is commonplace. Terry Wogan's Children in Need appeals on television in the 1980s and the highly successful *Blue Peter* charity appeals are good examples. Jimmy Savile is well known for his charity work for Stoke Mandeville Hospital. His appeal to raise £10,000,000 included the use of a variety of badges. 'I helped Jim fix it for Stoke Mandeville' appears in at least two sizes. Industry often lends a hand in exchange for publicity: 'I've helped Jimmy Savile's Stoke Mandeville Appeal—Duplicolor' and 'I fixed it for Jim with Macleans'—are part of the campaign which raised £250,000. Similar late 1970s badges are 'I helped Brian Rix and Kentucky Fried Chicken raise £15,000 for the Holiday Home for the Handicapped', and 'Bob's Barnados buses, are you helping' (Bob Monkhouse) were produced.

Appeal fund badges also indicate trends in the methods of raising cash, from the prewar carnivals to the sponsored walks, swims and, in the early 1980s, marathons and half-marathons. The London marathon alone is said to raise millions of pounds just from the individuals who complete the course. A further trend has been the sponsorship of daring stunts or similar events which attract media attention and therefore raise more money. Parachute jumps, mountain climbing, and crossing the globe have been some of the ways of doing this. The Stop Polio Campaign crossed the globe in two minis in 1979–80 to raise money for the cause.

Sometimes an appeal fund actually becomes a registered charity. The National Kidney Research Fund which began in 1965 is now a registered charity.

Throughout the 1950s and 1960s many local campaigns to raise money for X-ray machines took place, most of which issued a 1 in (25 mm) badge. Other more localized charities include those for hospices; LOROS, the Leicester Organisation for the Relief of Suffering, is one such example.

Reactions to the plight of the Third World, brought to our attention with such impact by television programmes about drought and starvation, produced a response by rock stars in 1984. Initiated by Bob Geldof, a group of stars under the name Band Aid produced a charity record which set a trend. In 1985 it was followed by the hugely successful 'Live Aid' concert which in Britain alone raised at least £40,000,000 for Africa. George Harrison, formerly of the Beatles, had done a similar thing in 1972 when he organized a concert at Madison Square Garden for the relief of famine in Bangladesh.

Appeal funds

1 A children's home appeal
2 and 3 X-ray campaigns of the early 1960s
4 and 5 Two early National Kidney Research Fund badges. The NKRF began in 1965
6 Badges worn by walkers in the 1981 Ten Tors expedition. They raised funds for a kidney machine for Plymouth Hospital
7 to 9 Many designs were issued in 1979 featuring the logo for the International Year of the Child. 9 is a Westfield moulded plastic paint-filled design
10 The Royal Institution for the Blind became the Royal National Institution for the Blind in 1948 so this badge may be prewar (White and Lambert)
11 Sponsored walks became very popular in the late 1960s. This Christian Aid walk was 24 miles
12 1972 Bangladesh badge
13 and 18 Well-known faces help raise funds. Bob Monkhouse (*18*) was helping to get buses for Barnardos in 1979 (a lithograph)
14 to 17 Early 1980s local hospice appeals. LOROS is the Leicestershire Organisation for the Relief of Suffering
20 Part of a £1,000,000 fund-raising scheme for research into child medicine
21 In 1984 the *Sun* newspaper was appealing for ½p coins which were to be phased out in 1985. By 1985 £1,500,000 had been raised
23 and 24 Part of Jimmy Savile's £10,000,000 appeal for the Stoke Mandeville Hospital in the early 1980s
25 Live Aid. Bob Geldof organized this appeal, and raised over £40,000,000 for Africa famine relief. The badge was made up by B Sanders and Sons for West Country Marketing

Individual charities

Save the Children Fund

Founded in 1919 with the goal of aiding children in need worldwide, in 1984 the Save the Children Fund operations cost more than £37,000 a day. It is estimated that in its first 65 years it raised £100,000,000. Various standard badge issues include a child half-clothed on a yellow background. This logo was used on both enamel and 1 in (25 mm) button badges, until it was replaced in the 1970s by the modern design of a stylized child with arms raised, in red. Children dancing round the globe is another design that appears on 1 in (25 mm) button badges before 1970.

The Roundabout and Act Club (1964–82) has two badges: the Roundabout badge had a rocking horse design and the Act badge simply said 'Act'. In 1980 SCF produced a booklet, *Multi Cultural Britain*, coinciding with a multi-cultural event in Hyde Park, and a $2\frac{1}{4}$ in (57 mm) badge was issued, 'Multi- Cultural Britain'.

NSPCC

The NSPCC was founded in 1884 with the aim of 'Preventing the public and private wrongs of children and the corruption of their morals; to take action for the enforcement of laws for their protection.'

In 1979 the Children's League of Pity became the NSPCC Young League. Groups who raised money were given 'medals' according to the amount they raised. For example a 50p medal was a 1 in (25 mm) button badge with a bluebird on a silver background. In 1980 there were 16 'medals' in all, including five 1 in (25 mm) button badges and 11 metal or enamel badges, the highest award being a £100 'medal'. By 1985 there were 24 badges, the highest award being for raising £750. In 1984 the centenary celebrations included a 1 in (25 mm) button badge with a cheeky cartoon-style happy bluebird in the centre.

RNLI

The RNLI was founded in 1824. In 1983, running their 258 lifeboats cost the RNLI £17,000,000. All of this money had to come from voluntary contributions. Many badges, of various sorts, have been used to raise funds. In 1982 a rectangular set of four designs were produced: the Arun, Atlantic 21, Waveney, and D Class. They have sold in very large numbers. In previous years a button badge was normally sold featuring the lifeboat, and at least five different designs are known. A moulded plastic lifeboat badge is also in existence, along with an older 1 in (25 mm) button badge featuring a life-belt. Local lifeboat stations have also issued their own badges, and Colourmaster produced some of these in the late 1970s. Appeal badges, such as 'I support the Nottinghamshire Lifeboat appeal' can also be found.

Help the Aged

The Help the Aged youth campaigns began in 1961, and over 20 button badges have been produced for this. Many of these are $1\frac{1}{4}$ in (32 mm) lithographed designs with 'Help the Aged' and 'Youth Campaign' in a band across the design, and in a variety of colours. Other variations are 'Youth Campaign—I am supporting Help the Aged' and 'Support Group Help the Aged Youth Campaign'. In 1982 at least two twenty-first anniversary lithographed badges were produced.

Name charities

1 to 3, and 8 to 10 Save the Children Fund badges. *1* is for the Roundabout Club, made up by White and Lambert. *2* is a logo design button badge, pre-1970. *3* is a logo design enamel. *9* was produced for the Stop Polio campaign launched in 1979. *10* was issued with Matey Bubble Bath in 1982, with a Baynham and Stanfield inner ring clip

4 to 7 The Children's League of Pity was adopted as one of the NSPCC's fund-raising groups as long ago as 1891. The Bluebird of Happiness was the logo of this group and was used on many of their badges. Marples and Beasley produced thousands of 'The Children's League of Pity' circular enamels. *4* is a Marples and Beasley enamel. *5* is a White and Lambert button badge. *6* are badges by W O Lewis used in conjunction with fund-raising by the NSPCC Young League

11 to 19 RNLI designs. *11* is moulded plastic. *12* is a 1960s design. *14* is by White and Lambert. *15* is by Colourmaster. *16* is one of a set of four 1981 oblong designs. *17* and *19* are 1970s designs. *18* is a 1980s design

20 Surf Lifesaving Club 1960s badge

21 to 25 Help the Aged. A cartoon dog called Hector was adopted for their 'Hector club' and at least three designs feature Hector in a variety of colours. Apart from these youth campaign badges there are also a number of plain 'Help the Aged' badges in different colours. All except *24* are lithographs; *24* is a White and Lambert crimp

26 The SAGA Club organizes holidays for the elderly. As well as this enamel, button badges also exist

1

2

3

4

5

6

7

8

9

10

11

12

13

14

15

16

17

18

19

20

21

22

23

24

25

26

Oxfam

Oxfam was formed in 1942 as the Oxford Committee for Famine Relief. By 1985 it was a highly organized charity. During the 1970s Oxfam opened a chain of charity shops in major towns and cities, staffed by volunteers, 15,000 to date.

Others

Dr Barnados, founded in 1866 as a child help charity, have 1 in (25 mm) button badges 'Barnado Helpers' (1970s) and 1 in (25 mm) badges with 'Barnado Helpers League' showing a boy pointing (1950s) as well as earlier enamels. The Arthritis and Rheumatism Council for Research (ARC) founded in 1937 and needing to raise £4,000,000 a year have a $1\frac{1}{4}$ in (32 mm) standard logo design.

The National Fund for Research into Crippling Diseases under the guise of Action Research was founded in 1952. Button badges with their flower logo are not uncommon. A more recent charity is the Riding for the Disabled founded in 1969. Several button badges have been issued, including a set from the Barrow Farm Group featuring the Exmoor ponies Honey, Pipkin and Minnie. The British Heart Foundation was founded in 1961 and in 1983 needed to raise £6,000,000 from voluntary contributions. As well as button badges a square plastic badge was produced in 1983 featuring their logo.

War on Want, founded in 1952 to deal with poverty in Britain and worldwide, have issued 1 in (25 mm) button badges for their 'junior army'. The National Children's Homes, founded in 1867, have also issued badges, including a 1983 'I'm a Sunny Smiler' $1\frac{1}{2}$ in (38 mm) badge, designed by 'English Life'.

Cancer Research Campaign began in 1923, and its many local branches, have produced badges such as the 'Yorkshire Cancer Research Campaign', a $1\frac{3}{4}$ in (45 mm) 1980 design.

Groups such as the Red Cross (founded 1870) and the St John's Ambulance Brigade (founded 1877) have many official and uniform badges. They have also used promotional badges such as 'The Red Cross Cares OK!' and 'Who cares? The Red Cross does' 1983, $2\frac{1}{8}$ in (55 mm) as well as the traditional enamel lapel badges.

The Queen Alexandra Hospital Home (1919) and the Royal British Legion (1921) are just two of the groups set up to aid ex-servicemen and their families. Both have issued badges. The British Legion designs are fairly common in enamel, but they are better known for their Poppy Day appeal. The Queen Alexandra Hospital Home have used button badges for many of their appeals, often awarding them as prizes for raising funds.

The Women's Voluntary Service was founded in 1938 and members carry out welfare work in the community, such as providing meals on wheels for the elderly and handicapped.

There are hundreds more groups worthy of mention. These include: Guide Dogs for the Blind, MENCAP, The Migraine Trust, The Spastic Society, The Variety Club of Great Britain, Invalid Children's Aid Association, Action in Distress, Royal National Institute for the Blind and Deaf, ('Make friends with a deaf child' is a $1\frac{3}{4}$ in (45 mm) button badge, and a big seller), PHAB, Shelter, Rotary International, The Samaritans, Radio Lollipop, Sailors Children's Society, Campaigns against Muscular Dystrophy, Cystic Fibrosis and Spina Bifida.

Name charities

1 to 3 Barnardo Helpers. *1* is an early enamel. *2* is a solid back gilt brooch made by Thomas Fattorini Ltd in the 1950s. *3* a 1980s design
4 and 10 Both White and Lambert crimps. The Migraine Trust (*10*) was founded in 1965 to raise funds to promote research into the causes, treatment and care of migraine sufferers
5 and 18 Women's Voluntary Services badges illustrating some of their community work. The WVS became the WRVS in 1966
6 and 12 Guide Dogs for the Blind was founded in 1931. *6* is a design used over a period of at least 20 years from the 1950s onwards
7 War on Want campaign against world poverty began in 1952. This design is from the 1960s
8 1980 Oxfam design for those who gave something to one of their shops
9, 19 and 20 Ex-servicemens' charities. *9* is from the 1970s. *19* and *20* were both made by J R Gaunt, then of London
11 The Arthritis and Rheumatism Council for research was founded in 1937. This logo design is from 1980
13 'Smily' fights multiple sclerosis
14 Age Concern was founded in 1940 and this is a Thomas Fattorini Ltd badge for junior helpers, 'The Forget-me-not Club'. An enamel 'Forget-me-not' club badge exists for women in domestic service
15 The Sailors Children's Society helps with the care and upbringing of orphaned children of seafarers. This is a 1970s design
16 Round Table stick pin by H W Miller Ltd
17, 29 and 30 St John's Ambulance Brigade. *7* is a war service enamel. *30* is one of a 1983 set of four
21 Riding for the Disabled Association was founded in 1969
22 Cancer Research Campaign was founded in 1923. This Yorkshire design is of the early 1980s
23 This Scottish enamel bears an unusual Fattorini address—Fattorini, Glasgow
24 The Variety Club of Great Britain have provided thousands of minibuses or 'Sunshine' coaches to worthy groups since the 1960s
25 1976 Action Research design
26 Late 1970s Spastics Society
27 Leukaemia Research Fund enamel, founded 1960
28 Red Cross design of 1983

Religious groups

Traditional designs

The decline in church-going since the war has resulted in a decline in the many varieties of metalled and enamelled badges. Through the 1920s and 1930s many hundreds of designs were made for Sunday schools, including ones for attendance, scripture examinations, punctuality, good conduct, and merit. Choirs, guilds, social clubs, boys' clubs, brotherhoods, sisterhoods, conferences, pilgrimages and missions all warranted the wearing of a badge. The Fattorini companies were once again among the main manufacturers. Apart from local groups, national organizations such as the Mothers Union, the Salvation Army, Young Men's and Women's Church Associations, The Church Army and Scripture Union, among many others, have all issued badges.

Button badges were also used frequently before the war and one of the earliest producers, The Merchants Portrait Company of London, issued many designs, often with a heavy use of gold colours. The 'From Sea to Sea Missionary Exhibition—Steward' badge is a good example of this. Sometimes, badges were in interesting shapes, such as one for the third Anglo-Catholic Congress July 1927. Precious metals were occasionally used such as silver, as in the 'Womens Union Diocese of Salisbury' design.

Button badges featuring texts from the Bible have been issued by Sunday schools and missions certainly since the 1950s. One early set made by G J G Ltd, London actually numbers the designs on the back; at least 15 of these 1 in (25 mm) designs are known. They were followed in the early 1960s and 1970s by a large similarly designed set of at least 24 badges. These badges were reissued over a period of at least 20 years, possibly by different companies. Later issues have 'P and I British Manufacture' on the rear; earlier ones were made by White and Lambert. The simple but effective designs feature the text around the edge of the badge and an illustration in a circle in the centre. One of the commoner 1960s designs is 'Church of England Sunday School Member', with a yellow cross radiating light in the centre.

The Kings Messengers and the Young Crusaders are just two examples of groups for older children, and many of these have issued metal and enamel rather than button badges. Other good examples are various enamels produced for churches such as Elim, and evangelical groups.

Religious groups

Religious badges vary from the sober, traditional designs to more colourful modern examples.
1 to **5**, **7** A variety of early religious button badges mostly from the 1920s. Notice the strong use of gold in many designs. *1*, *4* and *7* are all by the Merchants Portrait Company, London. *3* is a rare oval design
6 Scripture Union design
8 Mothers Union enamel
9 Church of England's Christian Family Year 1962–3 stick-pin design
10 and **19** Girls Friendly Society, a 1920s and 1930s Church of England organization
11 Church of England Mens Society badge made by H W Miller Ltd
12 Six evangelical enamels including some issued by Elim
13 1960s Kings Messengers, Church of England
14 Youth for Christ enamel by W O Lewis (Badges) Ltd
15 Young Crusaders enamel
16 Silver badge of the Womens Union in the Diocese of Salisbury (1920s)
17 and **18**, **20** to **22**, **31** to **33**, **35** to **37** Badges for a variety of Bible reading clubs or Sunday schools
23 A United Beach Mission design from Lyme Regis beach in 1983
24 to **26** From a set of 1950s Bible text designs sold in churches or Sunday schools and published by GJG Ltd, London
27 to **30** From a set of at least 24 Bible texts from the 1960 onwards period, published by P & I and still being issued in 1985
38 to **41** 1970s loudly coloured designs sold to youth groups and in religious book shops
42 Salvation Army commemorative badge

Modern religious designs

Whereas symbols such as Scripture Union's lamp or the cross are traditional religious designs, in 1971 another symbol emerged which was to become well used not only on religious badges but on a host of others as well. This was the smiling face, which originally appeared on a yellow background.

The 'Smily Face' originated in the United States, part of the 'Have a nice day', 'God loves you' craze, which lasted for about three years. In 1971 the Romford firm Anabas bought the licence for the design from an American company and registered it in this country. Anabas produced millions of 'Smily Faces' during a nine-month craze. 'Smile, Jesus loves you' was a common slogan, along with 'Jesus saves'. The smiling face appeared on a multitude of badge designs, in many sizes, and later in many colours. There were many bootlegs.

Another popular symbol was the pointing finger, sprouting a cross, with the slogan 'One way' underneath. This was produced in a variety of sickly colours in the early 1970s and in various sizes. Some badges were lithographs rather than acetates.

Sets of Bible texts were also issued. These included a 'Jesus said' set of $1\frac{1}{4}$ in (32 mm) buttons with a cross in the centre; at least eight examples are known. Around 1979 Colourmaster issued a set of six of their photographic designs (coded BLN 15–20). One of these features the slogan 'Jesus saves', this was satirized as 'Brian saves' when the Monty Python Film, *The Life of Brian*, created a stir. In the 1970s, with the growing interest in alternative religions, Tantra Designs produced sets of at least 50 designs in various sizes, as well as a set of 16 Celtic illustrations. These were often worn for the sake of fashion rather than faith. The 'Kells', as they were known, were based on ancient Celtic spiral and knot designs taken from stone and metal artefacts as well as from illuminated manuscripts.

A variety of Bible weeks, beach missions and pilgrimages produced badges in the 1970s and 1980s but, whereas years before these would mostly be of enamel or metal, plastic and buttons were now used. UBM, the United Beach Missions, and other such groups work on many beaches during the summer months and issue many badges. An increasing number of religious book shops were the outlet for religious badges in the late 1970s. New sets, either featuring a Bible text or similar slogans, were produced.

Rastafarianism, based on back-to-Africa beliefs of Marcus Garvey, emerged in Britain in the 1970s. Red, gold and green are the colours of the faith and the 'dreadlocks' hairstyle is also characteristic. Many badges exist using the three colours, sometimes carrying a political message and often featuring Bob Marley or Haile Selassie, or simply 'Smile'.

The views of the Roman Catholic Church on abortion and the pill provoked protest badges, such as the one from the feminist movement stating, 'Pope? nope'. 'If the Pope could get pregnant—abortion would be a sacrament' was a square design featuring a pregnant Pope. The gay movement issued a set of five protest badges. One simply says 'Religion is the problem, not the answer', while the other four feature the Pope with the slogans 'Carry on Breeding', 'Oh Karol Rights before rites', 'Rome or reason', and 'What! Not another Roman in Britain'. The last slogan relates to the play that was causing an outrage at that time.

Modern religious badges and alternative designs

1 to **6** The Smily face was adopted for all types of badges, many religious in their intention, others simply fashionable. *3* bears the 1971 copyright of Anabas. *4* is a lithograph. *2* and *6* were made up by White and Lambert

6 to **8** Rastafarianism, the Back to Africa religion, has flourished since the early 1970s

9 Example from the Celtic paintings set by Tantra Designs, mid-1970s

11 Example of the 'Tantra' set by Tantra, mid-1970s

12 1970s church design

13 One of a set of six by Colourmaster

14 In 1980 the Monty Python anti-religious film 'The Life of Brian' caused a stir, hence this design

15 to **17** Pilgrimage designs. *16* is a Westfield moulded plastic design. *17* is a White and Lambert 1980 badge

10, and **18** to **26** In 1982 the visit of Pope John Paul II was big business. At open-air rallies of as many as a quarter of a million people, many badges were sold. Three button badges were issued with the official logo, as well as one metal-backed badge with a second surface printed disc. *18* and *20* are official designs. *22* is a glitter design. *23* and *26* were issued by the womens' movement attacking the Pope's views on abortion. *10*, *24* and *25* are part of a set issued by a gay rights group

1

2

3

4 SMILE JESUS LOVES YOU

5

6 HAPPY DAYS

7 ROOTS

8 Smile

9

10 RELIGION IS THE PROBLEM NOT THE ANSWER!

11

12 CELESTIAL CHURCH OF CHRIST ELEPHANT & CASTLE · LONDON SE1

13 Jesus Saves

14 BRIAN SAVES

15 Pilgrim S-t-to Albans 1983

16 3-10 JUNE PILGRIM 83 SALISBURY CATHEDRAL

17 YOUNG ADVANCE 80 HEREFORD DIOCESE

18 POPE JOHN PAUL II BRITISH VISIT 1982

19 Pope John Paul II Wales '82

20

21 John Paul II our Pope WELCOME TO ENGLAND 1982

22

23 POPE? nope

24 carry on preaching

25 WHAT? NOT ANOTHER ROMAN IN BRITAIN

26 IF THE POPE COULD GET PREGNANT... ABORTION WOULD BE A SACRAMENT

Sports—enamel and metal badges

Millions of badges have been produced for sports clubs, both amateur and professional, local and national, since the late nineteenth century. The vast majority of these are enamels. Many are highly sought after, particularly the decorative prewar designs, and scores of specialist collectors exist for each different sport.

In the 1970s the cheaper types of imitation enamel badge flooded this market. Serious collectors steer clear of these, preferring the official club badges and supporters' club badges. Football club badges are a case in point. The spectator of the 1970s demanded cheaper badges and more of them and apart from the imitation enamels, many plastic and button badges also exist.

Enamel badges can be found for just about every sport, including athletics, golf, football, darts, horse-riding, bowling, angling, rugby, cricket, tennis, swimming, motor sport, archery, speedway and even hang gliding. Football, bowls and speedway make the most use of enamels. Manufacturers often produce a standard sport design with space for the name of the club.

Sports associations often issue badges too, particularly for school schemes. The Amateur Swimming Association personal survival tests have been going strong for many years and the number of children gaining awards and badges must run into the millions. The bronze, gold and silver designs are relatively common, but the 'honours' badge is rare. By 1975 the enamel badges were replaced by second surface printed discs on a metal back. By 1985 there were many more swimming schemes, awarding metal badges as well as the sew-on variety. The Amateur Athletics Association five-star award scheme, popular since the late 1970s, issues thousands of badges for the variety of awards. Many other schemes exist in schools and colleges, often including enamel or metal badges as awards.

Archery

There are over 600 archery clubs in Britain and well over 60 per cent of these have produced badges, many with target faces, arrows and bows, and with mysterious initials such as SCAA (Somerset County Archery Association).

Bowls

In 1985 there were 3,905 bowls clubs, and nearly all of these had a club badge. Moreover, when supplies run out a new club badge is often issued. Apart from the standard club designs, badges are issued for regions, districts, counties, nationals, club tours, international tours, tournaments, centenaries, league and other special events. Some badges date back to the nineteenth century and these are avidly collected by specialists. Some designs feature the letters F D F, which stands for the Francis Drake Fellowship.

Sports club badges

A page from Thomas Fattorini Ltd 1939 catalogue illustrating the range of enamel badges available for sports clubs.

BADGES for SPORTS CLUBS

Most of our National Sports Clubs have their own exclusive Badge, of which they are rightly proud. Members like to wear such Badges without which they feel "lost" almost as an outsider.

Let us design a special Badge for YOUR Club and you will be surprised at the extra keenness and enthusiasm it will create. There is no obligation in asking for designs and estimates.

THOMAS FATTORINI LTD. REGENT STREET WORKS BIRMINGHAM, 1

PLEASE NOTE THE **THOMAS** IN OUR NAME AS SIMILAR FIRMS ARE **NOT** THE SAME

Football

Such badges as the oval 'Accrington Stanley Division III' manufactured by Vaughton's and the circular football design 'Clapton Orient' by Miller's are what every enamel football badge collector longs for. The standard 'ball' badges were made for over 100 clubs by H W Miller Ltd of Birmingham. The Association of Football Badge Collector's excellent catalogue for 1983 listed over 1,700 'proper' enamel badges for clubs, supporters' clubs, junior supporters' clubs, anniversaries, associations, officials and victories, including non-league clubs. Since over 25 enamel badge manufacturers have produced these, being a collector is no easy task.

Speedway

Speedway, or dirt-track racing as it was originally known, originated in Australia and was introduced to Britain in 1927. By 1963 there were 24 British tracks and each of these issued enamel badges. It is a spectator sport with a cult following, the type that likes to collect badges. Speedway badges are different from other motorbike badges: manufacturers have issued standard designs for clubs. These include the 'crash helmeted heads' design.

Cycling

In 1985 in England and Wales alone there were 800 cycling clubs affiliated to the RTTC, Road Time Trials Council. Each one of these clubs probably issues a badge of some description, and many of them are enamel. Since the earliest days of cycling and the first club, the Pickwick Bicycle Club founded in 1870 in Downs Hotel, Hackney, thousands of club badges have been produced.

Motor racing and horse racing

The Isle of Man TT and similar motorcycle races issue enamel badges, as do other motor sports. Race tracks have badges for their members. Marples and Beasley manufactured many for the Mallory Park Members Club, which today are reminders of the many races that once took place on that racetrack.

Another large group of enamels are the horse-racing badges, many made by Lewis of Birmingham, for members of tracks such as Sandown and Newmarket. Some of these badges date from the last century.

Olympics

Metal and enamel designs were produced for the 1908 and 1948 Olympic Games, held in Britain, and they are very collectable. Other Olympic enamels include later examples made to support particular events, such as the British Equestrian team.

Sports—enamels

Sports badges are popular with collectors.
1 to **14** Postwar metal badges, all enamelled except *13* which is a much scorned second-surface printed insert of the late 1970s. *4* and *7* are by Coffer, London. *9* and *12* are by A E W, Birmingham. *6* is the well-designed Association of Football Badge Collectors enamel made by Parry of Birmingham
15 to **19** Postwar Speedway designs. *15* to *18* were made by W Reeves and Company, Birmingham. *19* is a second-surface printed insert and is unusual in that it bears a maker's name, Davis Badge Company of London
20 to **25** Postwar Bowling club designs. *20*, *22* and *23* were made by H W Miller Ltd. *21* is by Conroy Gough, Torquay, probably a shop
26 to **28** Angling badges. *26* is the York District Angling Society. *27* is a standard design of R E V Gomm with a club's initials added
29 and **30** Swimming designs. *30* is a common design along with bronze and silver awards; honours is rare. These became second-surface printed in the late 1970s
31 Curling club design by Thomas Fattorini Ltd
32 Olympic equestrian supporters design made by W O Lewis (Badges) Ltd
33 Second-surface printed insert for the 1979 York Cycle rally badge
34 and **35** Isle of Man TT race designs
36 and **37** Mallory Park club members' badges made by Marples and Beasley of Birmingham
38 Sailing design
39 and **40** Rugby Union and Rugby League designs
41 British Ski School award
42 British Hang Gliding Association, second-surface printed insert
43 Three As athletics award scheme badge of 1983

80

Football—button and plastic badges

Since the 1960s, button and plastic badges of individual footballers have become more popular as the star status of players has increased. The advertisements in the 1960s' editions of *Charles Buchans Football Monthly*, a magazine with its own boys' club badge, reveal a roaring trade in lapel badges. These were either button badges, often from David Stacey Publications, or as plastic lapel badges with a photographic disc in the centre (star-shaped). Hundreds of these were available from the New Manchester Programme Shop.

In those days, England had a world-beating team. When the 1966 World Cup final was held in England, the mascot 'World Cup Willie' was adopted by the Football Association (copyrighted 1965). All manner of Willie souvenirs were produced: stickers (2/–), pennants (6/6), pencils (9d), ties (15/6), car cushions (13/6), miniature boots (6/–), wall shields (15/–), raincoats with 'England for the World Cup' on the chest (£1), keyrings (6/6), miniature mascots (7/9), and a variety of lapel badges. A 1 in (25 mm) badge featuring Willie was the most popular, and at sixpence it was one of the cheaper souvenirs. A pin-on plastic cut-out Willie was (1/6), the height of one-upmanship in the schoolyard.

World Cup years have usually been marked by some type of mascot, which often features on badges. In 1982 England chose Bulldog Bobby. The Spaniards had chosen and copyrighted their mascot for 1982 as early as 1979. The euphoria with which the Scots sent off their team to Argentina in 1978 proved short-lived when their team performed disastrously. Television advertising campaigns featuring the team were withdrawn, and Magic Ally the team manager became 'Tragic Ally'. Many button badges were produced including a set of at least eight designs with slogans such as 'Ally's Tartan Army'. In 1982 these became 'Jock's Tartan Army'.

George Best proved a highly controversial figure in the early 1970s. His antics got so much press coverage that people became sick of hearing his name, and $2\frac{1}{8}$ in (55 mm) badges saying simply 'George who?' were popular with certain fans.

As well as badges featuring players, and soccer's controversies, millions have been issued with teams' names and colours. In the early 1960s, $\frac{7}{8}$ in (22 mm) team badges featuring the team's colours and nickname could be bought from bubble gum dispensing machines outside newsagent's shops. In the 1970s $2\frac{1}{4}$ in (57 mm) badges were available, many reflecting the new type of football supporter with designs such as 'Magic reds' showing a team scarf tied round the wrist, and 'Coventry magic WBA tragic'. Non-league clubs, too, often use button badges as they are easier on club funds and fans' pockets.

1

2

3

4 MICHAEL BAILEY

5 GORDON MILNE

6 CHARLES BUCHAN'S FOOTBALL MONTHLY BOYS' CLUB

7 BOSTON UNITED F C

8 THE REDS LIVERPOOL

9 THE TOFFEES EVERTON

10 EVENING POST TERRY COOPER GREEN POST

11 SCOTTISH FOOTBALL LEAGUE

12 FINDUS Chosen for England BOBBY CHARLTON

13 WORLD CUP WILLIE

14 WORLD CUP

15 SPAIN '82 BULLDOG BOBBY

16 GEORGE WHO?

17 MAGIC ALLY

18 WORLD CUP JOCK'S TARTAN ARMY SPAIN 82

19 THE Sun ROBSON MUST GO

20 THE Sun CLOUGH FOR ENGLAND!

21 MAGIC REDS

22 SUPER SIDOLL

23 WATFORD ARE MAGIC LUTON TRAGIC

24

Other sports—button and plastic badges

Whether it be a participation badge proving that you've been energetic, or a supporter's badge showing your allegiance, or even an 'I was there' badge, it comes under the banner of sport. The funding of Britain's Olympic team has always been a problem, and many badges can be found to prove it. The 1¾ in (45 mm) 'British Olympic Day supported by the Daily Mail' (1979), 1½ in (38 mm) 'McVities Olympic Appeal' (1983–84), and 1¼ in (32 mm) 'I support British Olympics' (1972), are all part of the fund-raising. In 1977 children were encouraged to help 'Moscow Olly' by collecting tokens from certain products and holding sponsored events.

The craze of the early 1980s was the 'fun run' and many badges commemorate the blisters, pulled muscles, and joy of finishing. The popularity of fun runs stems from the televizing of the first London Marathon, now an annual charity event. Many other runs raise money for charity and badges mark the occasion.

Local sports clubs often opt for the cheaper button or plastic badge. Clubs for darts, snooker, table tennis, badminton and even the larger sports centres come into this category.

Ice skating has proved a popular pastime over the years and many badges still exist for rinks which have since disappeared. In the 1980s there has been a boom in roller skating, mostly in the form of roller discos. Badges featuring roller boots are worn by enthusiasts.

Speedway stars, just like soccer stars, are captured for ever on 2½ in (64 mm) badges, usually worn by female fans. Motorbike personalities like Barry Sheene, held a similar mass appeal. A plastic badge in the shape of the number seven with Barry Sheene in the centre is just one souvenir. Grand prix motor drivers also have their fans. In the late 1970s it was James Hunt, and his reputation as 'Hunt the Shunt' is illustrated on a 2½ in (64 mm) badge with an 'L' plate and the statement 'I taught James Hunt to drive'. 'Rhymney is the name rugby is our game' is an 1¼ in (32 mm) badge that shows the Welsh side of Rugby Union, but in 1982 it was the English front row that caused a sensation in the shape of Erika. Erika, a shapely young lady, decided to run onto the field of play—topless—causing a stir to say the least. A few games later, hundreds of badges asking 'Sod the rugby where's Erika?' were sold.

Cricket, like so many sports, owes a lot to television. With the televizing of one-day games in the late 1960s and early 1970s the game attracted many new fans and new viewers. Accordingly sponsors could see the advertising potential and the John Player League and Benson and Hedges Cup emerged. Later the Test Series became sponsored by Cornhill Insurance who have issued many commemorative badges mostly 2 in (50 mm). County cricket clubs have issued plastic, shaped county badges and buttons. Their sponsor in 1984, Britannic Assurance, issued a 2⅛ in (55 mm) design, 'Support your county cricket club'.

Many other sports and sporting occasions have their own button or plastic badges. Sports centres such as Crystal Palace, bike rides such as the London to Brighton rally, local judo clubs, ten-pin bowling, local swimming pools, orienteering, gymnastics and horse racing, have all done so. A special set was issued in 1977 featuring 'Red Rum' the famous Grand National winning horse of the 1970s.

Other sports badges

1 to 5 Olympic appeals. *1* is for the 1972 Games in Munich. *2* to *4* Various efforts for the 1980 games in Moscow; *2* is a White and Lambert, *4* is a Baynham and Stanfield. *5* was for the 1984 games in Los Angeles
7 A 1950s skating badge
8 A 1980s roller disco plastic shaped badge
9 Cycling is not so much in the limelight, but the Milk Race and its sponsors make sure of some publicity with badges.
10, 19 and **23** are White and Lambert crimps. *23* is a 1978 design
11 Lunar Emblem, Liverpool made this darts design
12 One of several designs for the sponsorship of test cricket by Cornhill Insurance
13 Sports centre design featuring champion ice skater Robin Cousins on an early rectangular design
14 Part of a set issued by Taylorscope through Baynham and Stanfield (inner ring clip) in 1977
15 Speedway star
17 A 1960s speedway button badge made by White and Lambert
18 A shaped plastic badge made by Banbury plastics
20 One of the many badges for the fun run craze of the early 1980s
21 Paint-filled plastic badge by Westfield Advertising

1
2
3
4
5
6
7
8
9
10
11
12
13
14
15
16
17
18
19
20
21
22
23

Transport—enamel badges

Badges produced by and for transport enthusiasts plot a large part of our industrial heritage. Before 1960, only club enamels were common. Since then the growth of interest in preserving old rail networks and waterways and the fascination with old engines of every kind, has generated a wealth of material.

Rail

When Beeching cut back the railway service in the 1950s he couldn't have realized what a nostalgia industry he was creating. By 1985 there were many preserved railways. Enamel badges of railway engines began with the giant locomotives of the 1930s, Gresley's A4 Pacific engines of the LNER, and Stanier's Coronation Scot locomotives of the LMS. After the war these badges continued to be popular with train spotters, but it was after train spotting had all but died out that the badges really took off. As the last steam engines were withdrawn from British Rail in the 1960s more badges began to appear. One company, Squires, was selling well over 150 designs in 1963 retailing at four shillings each. These included coats-of-arms of railway companies, side views of different locomotives and historic locomotives. Other manufacturers were busy, too, H W Miller and R E V Gomm in particular. Gomms actually specialized in transport badges and have produced thousands of different designs, featuring just about any locomotive, bus, tram, truck, car or motorccycle you can mention, as well as badges showing vehicles' emblems and badges of railway companies' coats-of-arms. These can be seen adorning the hats, jackets and scarves of the transport enthusiast at rallies up and down the country.

Others

The Motor Cycle Riders Association have rallies all over the country for which badges are made, many by Gladman and Norman. Other motorcycle groups, such as Hells Angels, are renowned for wearing swastikas and skull-and-crossbones badges as well as tamer designs. Organizations such as the Omnibus Society or the PSV Circle (Public Service Vehicle) sell club badges to members. Car clubs, such as the MG Owners' Club, continue to issue enamels.

Enamel transport badges

These highly decorative badges are prized by collectors.

1 1960s Leyland logo
2 Early 1960s Scammell enamel by Thomas Fattorini Ltd
3 Paint-filled stamped metal JCB design early 1980
4 Car enthusiast's enamel
5 Squire made this Townsend Thorensen enamel
6 One of several enamel airport mascots
7, 34 and **35** Railway insignia. *7* and *34* are enamel. *35* is a second-surface printed insert
8 The Public Service Vehicle Circle for bus enthusiasts
9 A second-surface printed 1970s insert into a formed metal box, unusual in that it bears a maker's name, Fattorini and Sons
10 Hornby modellers enamel badge
11 Daimler logo
12 MG logo
13 and **14** Colourful enamel designs of the Motorcycle Riders Association supplied by Gladman and Norman of Birmingham
15 T N Priest and Company Ltd enamel for the Dirt Bike 1982 rally
16 Bikers second-surface printed insert into a shaped metal base
17 From a set of 'classic car' designs, R E V Gomm
18 and **19** Older railway engine enamels by H W Miller Ltd
20 and **21, 23** to **29, 31** to **33**, and **36** to **40** A small selection of the thousands of enamels supplied by R E V Gomm of Birmingham, especially since 1975
22 Commemorative design for the Trent Bus Company
30 A second-surface printed insert diesel design

1
2
3
4
5
6
7
8
9
10
11
12
13
14
15
16
17
18
19
20
21
22
23
24
25
26
27
28
29
30
31
32
33
34
35
36
37
38
39
40

87

Transport—button and plastic badges

Rail

The Ian Allan train spotters and bus spotters clubs of the 1950s and 1960s are amongst the earliest to produce transport button badges. The Ian Allan Loco Spotters Club was originally founded by Ian Allan in 1944 as the ABC Loco Spotters Club. By 1947 there were over 15,250 members, who had to abide by the club rule 'not to trespass on railway property or hinder railway servants'. One badge was supplied free on joining, a 1¼ in (32 mm) plastic badge with safety-pin fastening. This came in the six regional colours; brown for Western region, green for Southern region, red for London Midland region, dark blue for Eastern region, tangerine for North Eastern region, and blue for Scottish region. As well as the plastic badge the design was also available in chromium, but this cost ninepence extra. In the 1950s the club issued a 1 in (25 mm) button badge which featured a steam locomotive. In the 1960s this was a diesel locomotive, a warship class engine: by 1971 the club was wound up. The badge for the Bus Spotters Club is rarer altogether, as are other early button badges for transport enthusiasts, although *The Wizard* comic did issue an 'I am a loco spotter' badge in the early 1960s, a 1 in (25 mm) button badge showing a steam engine.

As the number of preserved railways increased through the 1970s so too did the amount of badges. Desperate for funds to keep steam alive, and diesels too, the gift shop was a must for every preserved line. The button badge was a souvenir every child (or adult) could afford. Some of the bigger preserved lines, among them the Festiniog, the Severn Valley, and the North Yorks Moors, have issued a wide range of button badges featuring various locomotives.

Standard sets are also sold at most railway enthusiasts' venues. R E V Gomm issued at least five standard 1½ in (38 mm) designs, including the Royal Scot, Flying Scotsman, Aveling and Porter Traction engine, and Burrell Showmans Road locomotive. Later Rainbow Designs, London Emblem Company, issued a set of 2⅛ in (55 mm) steam engines in photo form. There are at least eight, including Blackmore Vale, Appledore, Gordon, Blue Peter, Sir Nigel Gresley, George Stevenson, Cookham Manor and the Flying Scotsman. In 1978 Rainbow Designs produced a Thomas the Tank Engine set. The anniversary of 150 years of railways (1825 to 1975) was the occasion for other designs to be issued.

The rise, and initial failure, of the APT, Advanced Passenger Train, and the demise of the Deltic diesel locomotives in 1981 rekindled interest in diesel engines. A set of at least 16 badges was produced, illustrating, in photographic form, the main classes of diesels on British Railways. At the same time British Railways were encouraging children from 5 to 14 to join the Rail Riders Club. An official club button badge was produced, initially in 2⅛ in (55 mm) and later in 1 in (25 mm) designs.

In 1984 *Rail Enthusiast*, a new magazine for diesel enthusiasts in particular, produced a set of four designs featuring a Class 33, Class 50, Class 58 and Class 73 locomotive.

Railway button badges

Badges for spotters clubs and rallies are often the button variety.
1 to **4** Ian Allan Spotters Clubs of the 1950s and 1960s. *1* is North Eastern Region tangerine. *2* is Midland Region red, and *3* is Western Region brown. *2* and *3* are plastic
5 A design probably issued with *The Wizard* in the 1950s
6 A badge with *Rail Enthusiast*. One of a set of four
7 to **28** Various rail and steam museums, rallies, societies or railways of the 1970s and 1980s. *11*, *13*, *16*, *17*, *18*, *21*, *25*, and *26* are all White and Lambert crimps
29 One of a set of at least eight steam engines issued by Rainbow Designs around 1980
30 One of a set of 16 diesel classes of 1980
31 BR's Rail Riders Club design of the early 1980s

1

2

3

4

5

6

7

8

9

10

11

12

13

14

15

16

17

18

19

20

21

22

23

24

25

26

27

28

29

30

31

Other transport badges

In a similar way to the rail badges but on a smaller scale, button badges for bus enthusiasts have developed since 1975. The Tramway Museum at Critch and the Trolleybus Museum at Sandtoft, along with a host of more local bus museums, came into being through the 1970s. Individual bus groups, who may only own one vehicle, have badges made to sell at rallies. Many of these badges are 'homemade', often photographic.

Canal holidays became increasingly popular throughout the 1970s and the Inland Waterways Association has wasted no time bringing out promotional badges such as 'Up the cut' and 'Carry on Canals'. A variety of canal trusts, along with waterways museums such as Stoke Bruerne and Canal Shardlow also issue many button badges.

The West Midlands is famous for its network of canals. In 1983 the West Midlands County Council issued a 3 in (77 mm) button badge, 'I'm all steamed up', featuring the steam-driven narrow boat, along with an attractive rectangular design, 'Canals of the West Midlands'. 'Real boaters do it in tunnels', 'I need locking up', 'Captain', 'First Mate', 'Tiller girl' are other whimsical designs for the canal enthusiast.

The numerous appearances by the Red Arrows aerobatic team at airshows during the 1970s and 1980s are also commemorated in badge form. Aircraft museums such as the Fleet Air Arm Museum at Yeovilton, the Shuttleworth Collection, and RAF Hendon Museum have their own designs, too.

Other transport badges

White and Lambert made many of these recent transport badges.
1 to **4** and **6** to **8** Bus, tram, and trolleybus museums and rallies, 1975 to 1978
5 Car owners club badge made up by York Community Bookshop
9 1983 London Transport Golden Jubilee design
10 Mini enthusiasts rally, 1984 commemorating 25 years of the Mini
11 to **15** and **19** Aircraft museums and displays, 1975 to 1985
16 to **18** and **20** to **23** Inland waterways museums and promotions, 1975 to 1985. *21* is one of a set of at least six designs

Advertising

To a certain degree, all lapel badges are a form of advertising. Badges specifically designed to sell products have been around for a long time—ever since badges were first produced. They have formed an integral part of many famous campaigns, and their use over the years highlights aspects of the development of the advertising business as a whole.

This section presents a summary of that development and then looks at a range of products and services that badges bring to our attention.

The early days of advertising (1896–1939)

At the turn of the century there was a rapid growth in the advertising business in Britain. Whereas in 1896 there were no manufacturers of advertisers' novelties, by 1906 there were 26, plus two advertising balloon-makers. During the same period the number of advertising agencies doubled.

The birth of the button badge in the United States in 1896 attracted advertisers almost immediately, and button badges have been used in growing numbers ever since. In Britain the earliest advertising button badges include those produced for the Edward VII coronation. Normally, these early buttons carried the advert on the paper insert, and this was still the case in 1935 when Gossages soap issued a Silver Jubilee badge with a paper insert, 'Gossages 1d dry soap still the best'.

Generally, however, before the Second World War, agencies preferred to use items of better quality to advertise products. Celluloid mirrors, made in the same way as button badges, but with a mirror inserted instead of a pin, were as popular as button badges in the 1930s. These mirrors, which could be slipped into a lady's handbag, feature prominently in manufacturers' catalogues for this period. The badges worn were mostly enamel. With the introduction of Robertson's golly in the 1930s, along with improved enamelling techniques, came a host of other company mascots.

One reason for the dearth of button badges could be that children were not in the habit of wearing badges in the 1920s and 1930s, but a more plausible reason is that the pattern of shopping, and hence of advertising, was different. The grocer of the 1920s and 1930s was responsible for choosing and pricing many of his goods. Competition was between grocers, not manufacturers.

With the advent of prepackaging, the skills of the grocer were no longer needed. Manufacturers insisted that their goods could not be sold below list price and took over the role of advising the public what to buy. The discount to the grocer was reduced, the extra money was spent on advertising and grocers were forced to stock the goods that the customer had seen advertised. This trend, which began before the First World War and continued unabated after 1945, increased the importance of advertising and, in turn, advertising's demand for new gimmicks like the button badge.

Early advertising badges

A selection of prewar enamel advertising designs by Thomas Fattorini Ltd, as shown in their 1939 catalogue.

ADVERTISING BADGES

Most of our large National Advertisers use Badges and the repeat orders we get prove their worth as useful advertising.

A nice Badge costing a few pence will be worn and seen for a very long time after all other kinds of advertisement are forgotten.

The cost of Badges is negligible compared with the advantages.

Ask us for a quotation and special sketches — there is no obligation.

THOMAS FATTORINI LTD. REGENT STREET WORKS **BIRMINGHAM, 1**

PLEASE NOTE THE **THOMAS** IN OUR NAME AS SIMILAR FIRMS ARE **NOT** THE SAME

93

The postwar boom (1945-70)

In the early 1950s, the end of rationing and the beginnings of commercial television, together with the underlying changes in the retail trade, helped to foster a badge boom. Advertising agencies made full use of every form of media: large hoardings were erected to hide bomb sites and button badges were also pressed into service. Ninety per cent of those issued from 1945 to 1965 are either 1 in (25 mm) or 1¼ in (32 mm).

While badges were mostly used during this period to advertise petrol and icecream, they also played a part in the launching of new products. Baby foods, and pet foods, in particular, developed in the 1950s and usually warranted big promotional campaigns. Cow and Gate baby foods boasted royal patronage with a 'Smiler league' logo. Dog foods, such as Vims and Spillers emerged, and slogans like 'Give him Benbows for a long life and a gay one'. The Wills Woodbine cigarettes badges are interesting reminders of the days when there were no restrictions on tobacco advertising.

The use of company mascots continued to be popular. 'Sifta Sam jolly good salt' (1 in/25 mm) and 'Mr Chip of Keiller' (1¼ in/32 mm) are good examples of this. It was in this period that Robertson's gollies achieved their peak of popularity.

Advertisers did not miss out on the tradition of issuing badges for clubs and awards. Wrights South Shields Biscuits Mischief Club' and 'Coco Road Safety Award Lyons Tea' are good examples. The League of Ovaltineys was advertised initially on Radio Luxemburg, which was a powerful medium (in 1954, one 15-word advertisement brought 229,000 replies). At least four badge designs are known from this campaign. The most common is a 1 in (25 mm) lithographed example (emphasizing the numbers produced) with the letters 'LO' in the centre.

The Festival of Britain in 1951 and the coronation in 1953 were two events that boosted British advertising. Neptune drinks issued a 1¼ in (32 mm) coronation badge in 1953. Similarly, the 'Buy British' campaign of the 1960s encouraged consumers to invest in British goods, just as they had done in the 1930s. 'I'm backing Britain' in 1968 proved one of the more successful campaigns. While crisps and chocolate bar markets grew tremendously in the 1970s and 1980s, the big campaigns began earlier. Smith's potato crisps issued a 1¼ in (32 mm) badge featuring their logo around 1960.

Via television the 'Bisto Kids' were reborn and the saying 'Ah! Bisto' became popular. A 1¼ in (32 mm) badge was issued. The Bisto Kids Club was also reformed in the late 1970s. The effect of commercial television was beginning to be seen.

General advertising designs from 1945 to 1970

Note the standard 1 in (25 mm) and 1¼ in (30 mm) designs and the relative lack of sophistication.
2 League of Ovaltineys designs over the years
5, 11, 19, 24 Designs by J R Gaunt and Sons Ltd
13 Coco the clown advertises Lyons Tea and safety
23 Archie Andrews, a ventriloquist's dummy that became famous on the radio in the 1950s, was used by Meddocream Ltd for this Lollie Club promotion in the mid-1950s

Advertising today

Throughout the 1970s advertising made use of more, bigger badges. The $\frac{7}{8}$ in (22 mm), 1 in (25 mm), and $1\frac{1}{4}$ in (32 mm) became scarcer in favour of $1\frac{1}{2}$ in (38 mm), $1\frac{3}{4}$ in (45 mm), 2 in (50 mm), $2\frac{1}{8}$ in (55 mm), and the 'frying pans'—$2\frac{1}{2}$ in (67 mm), 3 in (74 mm) and upwards. By 1985 the commonest sizes were $2\frac{1}{8}$ in (55 mm) and $2\frac{1}{4}$ in (57 mm), millions were being made for all manner of products.

New products included hard and software for the electronics industry and a vast range of 'junk' food. Outlets such as Wimpy and McDonalds operated a franchise system and spread all over the country, publicized by national advertising campaigns.

By 1970 nearly everyone had access to a television. Slogans and jingles which became famous on TV were reproduced on badges. The Brooke Bond chimps, the Dulux dog and Buzby were characters drawn from campaigns that swamped the media. Many of these saturation campaigns gave rise to 'anti' badges. The Esso 'Put a tiger in your tank' campaign provoked a 'Stuff the tiger' badge.

The use of cartoon characters has been more popular since 1968 and the revolutionary graphics by Heinz Edelman for The Beatles' animated film, *Yellow Submarine*. Character merchandising was in its infancy in Britain in 1970, but by 1980 it was a fully fledged business, and this is reflected in modern advertising badges.

Apart from the use of animals and cartoon characters, popular children's characters have been adopted in many designs. Muscleman and Superman variations abound, such as Fyffes Supernana ($1\frac{3}{4}$ in/45 mm). Monsters, space, and other comic themes crop up regularly.

Apart from button badges, which by 1985 made up at least 90 percent of this market, plastic, metal and card have all been used. Bassetts revitalized 'Bertie Bassett' in a metal design (1983), and Everready shaped their battery into a 'he man' in plastic.

Advertising badges are available from a number of sources: from shops and trade fairs; from the product itself; or from the manufacturers once enough 'tokens' have been collected. Sometimes the badge is for a 'club' connected to the product. Many firms sponsor environmental campaigns, notably Smith's and Golden Wonder, and the makers of Matey Bubble Bath. One of the originators of the token idea was Robertson's with their gollies, and they were still doing this in 1985.

Controls over advertising, issued by the British Code of Advertisement Practice, have regulated modern campaigns. Thus no badges featuring cigarettes have been made since 1970. Moreover, pressure groups for women's rights and racial equality have also affected designs. By 1985 the stereotyped housewife is harder to find, although the half-clothed female still appears in various situations. Occasionally badges cause a storm for other reasons. In 1984 Cadbury issued a mug-shaped plastic badge with their drinking chocolate. This badge looked so much like chocolate that viewers complained to *That's Life*, the BBC consumer programme, worried children may be tempted to eat the badge instead of wear it. It was duly removed.

Advertising today

Advertising today exploits the badge to the hilt.
1 A Mars a day . . . a late 1970s design
2 to **7**, **10** and **11** Popular cartoon-style characters include: Bertie Bassett (5), the Sugar Puffs honey monster (a card plastic badge) (6) and the Country Life buttermen (7). *10* is a 1981 shaped plastic badge; *11* a lithograph from the late 1970s
8 A short-lived badge issued with Cadbury's drinking chocolate. It was promptly removed after bad publicity on BBC TV's *That's Life*
9 Big computers mean big business and in 1981 meant big business. This is a 3 in (77 mm) frying pan
12 Another 3 in (77 mm) frying pan, this time for Mothers Pride bread
13 Space-shaped pasta promoted by Heinz in 1984
14 and **16** Square and rectangular computer badges reflecting new trends in 1983–4
15 Mr Gas, the blue flame, emerged in the mid-1970s
17 The energy crisis of the 1970s is reflected in this Electricity Board badge awarded to 'Energy Saving Homes', mostly in conjunction with Economy 7. The medallion award was still in use in 1985

Transport advertising

Petrol

Shell and BP 1 in (25 mm) button badges dating from the mid-1950s have become classics. Their reissue, up to at least 1962, has ensured that they are not uncommon. Variations include 'Super Shell', 'BP Plus' and 'BP Super Plus'. As early as 1939 Cleveland Discol and Mobiloil were using button badges, and throughout the 1950s and 1960s a steady stream of 1 in (25 mm), $1\frac{1}{4}$ in (32 mm) and $1\frac{1}{2}$ in (38 mm) badges were issued, for companies including: Jet, Vigzal, Fina, Regent, Globe, Mobil, Castrol, Thrust, Amoco, EP, Murco, ICI, Rix, Total, Cleveland and many others. The most famous petrol campaign of the 1960s was the 'Put a tiger in your tank' campaign by Esso. A set of four $1\frac{1}{4}$ in (32 mm) designs were issued: 'Put me in', 'Save the tiger campaign—drive generously', 'Bring back the cat' and 'Put him in—drive generously'. A follow-up to this campaign was the anti badge, 'Stuff the tiger'. Esso also issued plastic model Esso men on a chain, as well as plastic, shaped badges. The slogan 'Go well Go Shell' was issued as a square flickering badge.

Motor industry

Motor accidents were on the increase in the 1960s and 1970s and safety products, such as better tyres, were in fierce competition. Michelin with their Michelin man, have been keen badge users: at least 10 designs featuring the Michelin man have been issued since 1970. Other tyre firms and tyre centres feature on many badges, as do other components from batteries to wiper blades. Unipart are another keen user of badges in their promotions, and issued some notable 'frying pans' for their 'The answer is yes, now what's the question' campaign.

Many of the badges for car manufacturers can be found on trade stalls, often at events such as the Motor Show. British Leyland, Volvo and Ford have all been generous issuers of button badges. 'Ford Tractor Parts' was a set of at least four designs, given away at the Yorkshire Show in 1980. Such giveaways are usually accompanied by plastic bags, balloons, pens, hats and so on, and are very popular.

National Petrol were not giving anything away in 1977. They had spent enough popularizing the Smurfs and could afford to sell the badges featuring these creatures. A set of at least 12 $1\frac{1}{2}$ in (38 mm) and four 2 in (50 mm) designs with a yellow background were issued via National petrol stations. Since then, the Smurfs have become saleable products in their own right. Books, films and records featuring them were all accompanied by badges. Anti-Smurf badges and a record *Stamp on a Smurf* also became popular.

Public transport

Bus and train services have found an increasing need to promote themselves. 'This is the age of the train' promoted by Jimmy Savile featured the British Rail 125 high-speed trains which were introduced into the rail system in the mid–1970s. Several badges feature the 125 and its Inter City services.

In 1983 London Transport celebrated its Golden Jubilee and several badges were issued. Hawker Siddeley issued a $2\frac{1}{4}$ in (57 mm) badge, 'I've seen the secrets of keeping London on the move' during a big open day at their Chiswick Centre.

Transport

1 to 10 1950s and 1960s petrol and oil badges. *1* to *5* are classic 1 in (25 mm) 1950s designs, of which well over 15 are known. *6* is a plastic badge made to look like a tractor tyre. *7* is the shaped plastic Esso man. *8* is one of a set of four 'Put a tiger in your tank' designs. *9* is the alternative

11 A 1970s Texaco campaign; 'Hwyl' is Welsh for 'Have fun'

12 and 13 Smurf and alternative of 1977. *12* is one of a set of at least 16 designs sold at National petrol stations

14 1978 'Switch to Michelin' design

15 Shaped plastic 'Home Tune' man of 1984

16 One of many Ford designs. This one supplied by Hardisty Roll Badge Company, Harrogate and made up by Baynham and Stanfield around 1984

17 Mobil Oil 'Stamp out dinosaur thinking' badge

19 Car rental firms mushroomed in the 1970s and Budget issued a set of at least six designs. Budget rent-a-car, from a set in 1983–4

20 and 21 British Rail promotions 1979 to 1983

22 Leyland, too have used badges regularly in their promotions; this one is from 1983

23 Public transport has been the victim, far too often, of mindless vandals. South Yorkshire PTE led an anti-vandal campaign in 1983. The 'I don't take it out on my bus! It's my transport', $1\frac{1}{2}$ in (38 mm) was a clever design featuring a fist and a bus.

Food

Dairy products

The well-known slogan of the 1960s 'Drinka pinta milka day' was the result of harassed advertising copywriters' attempts to cram the message onto a poster using only four words. The campaign was devised by Mather and Crowther, one of London's most successful agencies. Three or more 2⅛ in (55 mm) designs, unusually large for that period, featured the follow up 'Ask me for an extra pinta', and a 1 in (25 mm) design stated simply 'I'm a pinta kid'. Later, in the 1970s, a stylized cow was adopted, complete with a flower on the end of its tail. Featuring this logo was a 2⅛ in (55 mm) badge saying 'Enjoy a pinta what you fancy'. Other slogans in the same series include a 1½ in (38 mm) 'Enjoy a natural pinta', 'I like milk', and 'Milk makes it naturally'.

Following on from the successful 'Drinka pinta milka day' the new slogan 'Milk has gotta lotta bottle' was an instant hit. Several badges have been issued, the standard one (1½ in/38 mm) features the new bottle shape and the slogan 'I've gotta lotta bottle'.

Cream campaigns include 'Saturday cat', a 1½ in (38 mm) design from the early 1970s. (This badge comes in two varieties; one where the cat has a red tongue and one with a white tongue.) The 'Go on be a devil—fresh cream' is a campaign of the late 1970s and 1980s. Local and national dairies have also produced many badges.

Flour

Some of the better-known food badges feature characters who became famous through television advertising. Fred and the Home Pride flour graders were first drawn in 1965. At that stage they had no arms. They were drawn by Tony Cattaneo who later added arms. The voice of John le Mesurier added to their credibility and they attracted much fan mail. Badges produced include a 1¼ in (32 mm) 'Home Pride needs you' (a la Kitchener), 'Thump a lump today', and 'Lord Mayor's Day 1974' (presumably for Spillers' float in the Lord Mayor's parade). Rainbow Designs issued some 2⅛ in (55 mm) badges in 1979, including 'Do you go in for regular self raising?'

Other food campaigns

The Spillers' flour grader has been called the most 'design perfect' character in commercial animation. Along with Cattaneo, three other men, Bob Geers, Bob Cross and Ron Wyatt formed a company on the basis of the Spillers' success. Other successes followed, all of which came in badge form. These included the Dunlop groundhog, Tetley tea folk, KP Crisp monks and the Country Life buttermen. The Buttermen feature on a yellow and black plastic design.

Other campaigns from the bakery include 'Nice one' from Wonderloaf, 'Mothers Pride I'm a loafer', 'Smile with Sunblest', and 'Hovis the wheatgerm bread'. The Hovis badge is 2¼ in (57 mm) and features a still from the superb series of nostalgic commercials by the British agency Collett, Dickenson, Pearce. Many local bakeries have also produced badges, especially since 1980, emphasizing the healthy wholemeal products.

Of the thousands of other food badges one that must be mentioned was issued as part of the campaign for British cheeses of 1983. This featured Mr Cheese who, complete with pinstripe suit, umbrella, and bowler was another use of the city gent, Fred the flour grader.

1 to 13 Dairy designs. The slick slogans from 'Drinka pinta milka day' in the early 1960s to 'I've gotta lotta bottle' in the early 1980s are illustrated here. *1* is from the early 1960s set, and has a solid back and safety pin. *2* is a Gaunt of Birmingham badge. *5* is an early 1970s cream promotion. This one has a red tongue, other Saturday cats do not! A stylized cow appears on many dairy promotions during the 1970s (*7*). *9*, *10* and *20* are by Westfield Advertising, made up by White and Lambert. *11* A short-lived promotion which was replaced by a new shaped bottle in *12*

14 to 16 Fred the Flour grader was the artwork of Tony Cattaneo and the voice of John le Mesurier

17 and 18 Compare the 1960s bread promotion (*17*) with that of the 1980s, taken straight from the nostalgia-ridden TV commercial (*18*)

19 1983 promotion for British cheeses

Drinks

Tea

The story goes that the famous PG Tips campaign in the 1950s was inspired by a trip to London Zoo. The first commercial was screened in 1956, and over the years the Brooke Bond chimps have become some of the best-loved characters on television. It is interesting that Peter Sellers voiced over that first commercial (receiving £100 for the job). Other stars such as Stanley Baxter, Fred Emney, Bruce Forsythe, Irene Handle, Arthur Lowe, Bob Monkhouse and Kenneth Williams have all contributed. Several badges have featured these famous chimps. An early 1½ in (38 mm) design is 'Brooke Bond PG Tips national favourite' on which the chimp's lips move. On a 1½ in (38 mm) badge, the slogan 'My name's Bond Brooke Bond' is taken straight from the 1980 commercial and a 2¼ in (57 mm) 'PG Tips chimps rule OK' is a variation on the OK theme. Other Brook Bond designs include 'Brooke Bond picture card collector' 1¼ in (32 mm), a reference to the popular giveaway cards.

Other teas such as Ringtons, Reddings, Lyons and even Darjeeling have all used badges. The Tea Council have also promoted tea on badges such as 'Tea's me' (2¼ in/57 mm) and 'All you need is tea' (1½ in/38 mm), clearly taken from *All You Need Is Love* by The Beatles and featuring psychedelic colours.

Cold drinks

The two American giants of the soft drinks trade, Pepsi-Cola and Coca-Cola, have been engaged in what has become known as the cola war since 1898. Their respective logos have become universal symbols of the American way of life, and their campaigns have been called the biggest marketing battle of all time. In the 1950s Pepsi Cola carried out a big advertising campaign to help establish their product in Britain. A bottle top design incorporating their logo, which is not unlike the Coca-Cola symbol, was put on a 1 in (25 mm) badge. Interestingly, the same design idea was used by Colt 45 some 20 years later on a 2¼ in (57 mm) badge.

Coca-Cola, in campaigns to distinguish itself from Pepsi and all of the others, stole a march in the early 1970s with 'Coke is it!' and 'It's the real thing'. The slogan was taken from their 1971 television commercial in which a multi-racial choir sang, 'I'd like to buy the world a Coke'. Both of the jingles, 'It's the real thing' and 'I'd like to teach the world to sing', were written by Roger Greenaway. Alternative badges, a sure sign that a campaign is a winner, were produced, including, 'Gay love—it's the real thing'. The slogan 'Enjoy Coca-Cola' was transcribed to 'Enjoy Cocaine'. The logo was popular enough to issue on a set of at least six 1 in (25 mm) badges, sold in gift shops, and featuring the logo in different languages in 1983.

In 1980 Unigate Dairies launched a promotion for 'Farmers Wife Pop'. With every bottle a free badge was given. There were six characters to be collected: Lofty Lime, Stix Lemon, Fats Orange, King Cola, Cherry Ade, and Soda Sax Junior. Other soft drinks campaigns that offered badges include: 'Cresta its frothy man', 'Tizer the appetizer', 'Adore a-Kia-ora', 'Crusha', 'Slush Puppie', 'Lido Slush', and 'Irn Bru'.

1 to 4 The Brooke Bond chimps became firm TV favourites. *1* is a 1960s design. *3* is a 1980s take-off of James Bond. *4* shows that 'Rule OK' slogan again

5 'All you need is tea' from the late 1960s

6 Late 1970s tea promotion

7 Lyons tea, taken from a late 1970s TV commercial

8 Early 1980s Nescafe design

9 and 14 Pepsi-Cola design of the early 1950s, adapted by Colt 45 in the 1980s

10 to 13 Coca-Cola and some of its alternatives. *11* is part of a set of at least six foreign translations sold in gift shops in 1983. *12* is reflective. *13* was published by Gay News

15 Although this badge is for 'Pepsi', 'Coke' were actually first on the diet scene

16 and 17 1960s soft drinks campaigns

18 to 22 1978 to 1985 soft drinks campaigns. *18* is part of a set of six, as is *20*

Alcohol

Brewery badges, worn by beer drinkers, were produced both before and after the war in enamel. The Guinness Company began advertising their stout back in 1928 when they ran a campaign in Scotland. In 1928 Guinness were in the unusual position of having the biggest brewery in the world, but not the system of tied public houses through which to sell their product. They were manufacturers pure and simple, and in 1928 they were prepared to spend vast amounts on advertising. Through the work of Oswald Greene of the Benson's agency they came up with the slogan 'Guinness is good for you', revolutionary for the period. Since the 1960s it has been illegal to imply alcohol can be 'good for you' in any medical sense and the 'Good for you' slogan has long been replaced by a series of adverts and slogans noted for their wit and humour. The success of the Guinness campaigns is clear through the popularity of alternative badges, such as 'Guinness makes you fart' of 1980, one in the Bristol Buttons set of 87.

Other breweries could not hope to match the spending power of Guinness, but enamels exist for all the big breweries, often featuring a mascot. William Youngers introduced a set of 'Father William' enamel designs much prized by collectors.

Since 1971 the Campaign for Real Ale, (CAMRA) has been successful in its campaign to force the big breweries to give the consumer 'real ale'. One example of CAMRA's excellent work was their 1978 campaign against John Smiths, the Tadcaster brewery. The badge featured the Courage cockerel and the slogan 'John Smiths it's fowl'. For several years John Smiths would not budge but by 1985 this large brewery was producing a real ale. A similar campaign was led against Bass, the Burton-on-Trent brewery, and a set of six badges were issued to 'Save our draught Bass'. CAMRA are also responsible for many beer festivals around the country and these often issue badges.

Between 1970 and 1985 breweries issued many sets of badges to accompany national advertising campaigns. These include those for Watneys Pale, a set of at least three to accompany their early 1970s Morecambe and Wise advert; Skol's Skolar set of four; the four for Russchian Vodka; Bulmers Cider; McEwans Lager; and those for William Youngers' Tartan—at least three sets, one featuring Father William. Discovering Smirnoff also became very popular in the 1970s and alternative badges exist for this well-worn slogan.

Alcohol

1 'Guinness is good for you', a prewar enamel by H W Miller Ltd, Birmingham
2 1979 alternative Guinness design by West Country Marketing and Advertising (Bristol Buttons)
3, 6, 9, 10, 11, 12, 14, 19, 20, and 22 Various alcohol promotions of the 1970s and 1980s. 6 and 11 feature 'Father William' of Youngers Brewery. Prewar enamels featuring Father William in various guises are greatly sought after
4 and 5 Bass Brewery badges. 4 is a Bass Brewery triangle lapel stud type
7 and 8 Both badges relate to John Smiths brewery. 8 is their Courage cockerel lapel pin. 7 is a 1978 Real Ale design attacking the John Smiths gassy beers. By 1985 even John Smiths were producing a real ale
13 A local Gloucester Brewery, made by White and Lambert, 1977
15 to 18 CAMRA badges, both local and national from 1971 to 1982
21 The Magnet Ales logo from John Smiths Tadcaster brewery

Confectionery and savouries

The sweet and innocent good guy, complete with National Health specs and blond hair sums up the image of the 'Milky Bar Kid', who, in the early 1960s, promoted Nestles' Milky Bar to great effect. The other Milky Bar badge was the luminous 'Milky Bar Kid nightrider'. In 1983 Nestles revamped the Milky Bar Kid—cowboys were out and spacemen were in—and 'Who shot the Milky Bar Kid into Space' featured the Milky Bar Kid on a $2\frac{1}{8}$ in (55 mm) plastic badge complete with a luminous rim (by Westfield).

Golden Wonder issued many badges from the early 1960s to the 1970s, when the shapes and flavours revolution saw a host of new products. Their Peanut Club came with a set of at least six 1 in (25 mm) badges: 'Chief P'nut'; 'I'm the p'nuttiest', 'Spaceman P'nut', 'Princess P'nut', 'Super P'nut', and 'P'nut 1st class'. These designs were printed both in red on white and white on red. 'The Nibb-it Savouries Club' (1 in/25 mm) was another early 1960s design. Others include those for Smiths crisps; three for Chipmunk crisps; 'I like Tudor crisps' featuring Henry VIII, and Walters Puffs, $1\frac{1}{4}$ in (32 mm).

By the late 1970s there were a host of new savoury products. 'Who stole my Hula Hoops' is a design which incorporated the Incredible Hulk, popular on television at that time. KP Nuts have produced many badges for their promotions.

Bubble gum and chewing gum were products which often gave away badges in the 1960s. A & BC gave away $\frac{7}{8}$ in (22 mm) badges of football teams, together with designs such as 'I hate school', and a set of Batman characters. The Bazooka Joe club had its own badge, a $1\frac{1}{4}$ in (32 mm) design featuring Bazooka Joe, a sort of Milky Bar Kid with eye patch. Anglo XL bubble gum issued 'A bubbly champ' ($1\frac{1}{4}$ in/32 mm). One of the best-known gum slogans, once again because of television, is 'Call it Wrigleys, call it spearmint, call it gum', a jingle written by Rod Allen (who also wrote 'The Wonder of Woolworths', 'Berger Berger', 'This is luxury you can afford by Cyril Lord', and 'Come and talk to the Midland', among others). A $2\frac{1}{8}$ in (55 mm) design features this late 1970s campaign. Double Agents sweets issued a set of badges featuring a black silhouette against four different backgrounds in $1\frac{1}{4}$ in (32 mm) and $1\frac{1}{2}$ in (38 mm) sizes.

'Polo, the Mint with the Hole' was famous enough to provoke a novelty alternative, 'I've got a hole with a mint', during the late 1960s.

During 1968 the Cadbury's Fruit and Nut Case campaign was in full swing complete with at least three badge designs, all $1\frac{1}{2}$ in (38 mm). Cadbury's promotions have usually been accompanied by badges. These include: 'Freddo', at least five $1\frac{1}{4}$ in (32 mm) designs; three 'Double Decker' designs; three 'Cadbury Flake' designs; 'Cadbury's monsters' $1\frac{1}{4}$ in (32 mm) lithographs; at least six 'Curly Wurly' designs; 'Cadbury's Bears'; 'Cadbury's Animals'; 'Cadbury's Welcome'; and a 1984 set promoting the new 'Wispa Bar'.

Rowntree's Jelly Tots promotion featured a set of five: 'I'm a Candy Tot', 'I'm a Teddy Tot', 'I'm a Jelly Tots Sentry', 'I'm a Tiger Tot', and 'I'm a Jelly Tot'. Their Yorkie campaign was aimed at an older age group and an enamel badge was issued. In 1973 it was 'Feed Aztecs to me' ($1\frac{1}{4}$ in/32 mm), and, in 1985, by sending Rolo wrappers, a set of four badges could be collected.

Snacks

Both sweet and savoury snacks have been the subject of fierce promotion. Badges are an important part of the attempt to win a market for a new product.
1 Luminous early 1960s 'Milky Bar Kid Night Rider' badge made up by J R Gaunt, Birmingham
2 Glow rim design by Westfield Advertising, early 1980s
3 1960s Milky Bar Kid badge
4 1978 Toffo badge
5 Clever Mars design of early 1970s
6 One of a set of four Rolo designs of 1985
7 Enamel issued during early Yorkie Bar promotion, 1978
8 One of a set of at least five for Freddo around 1974
9 Barratt's used Tom and Jerry in 1977 in a set of five
11 A badge promoting Jelly Tots, one of a set of five designs
12 Gaunt of Birmingham made up this Bertie Bassett in the late 1960s
13 Badge and Novelty Company have their name on the rim of this late 1960s alternative Polo badge
14 One of a set issued for the launch of Cadbury's Wispa bar in 1984
15 One of a set issued from bubble gum dispensers in the mid-1960s
16 to 20 Early 1960s crisp and savoury promotions. 16 is a Gaunt of Birmingham design. 19 is from a large set
21 One of a set of two 1979 designs for Hula Hoops using the 'Hulk' TV character. 'A typical Hula Hoops eater' was the other design, and the badge illustrated is actually a proof for the final design. 'Who stole my Hula Hoops?' was in red
22 Slogan from a jingle written by Rod Allen
23 and 24 Bubble gum badges

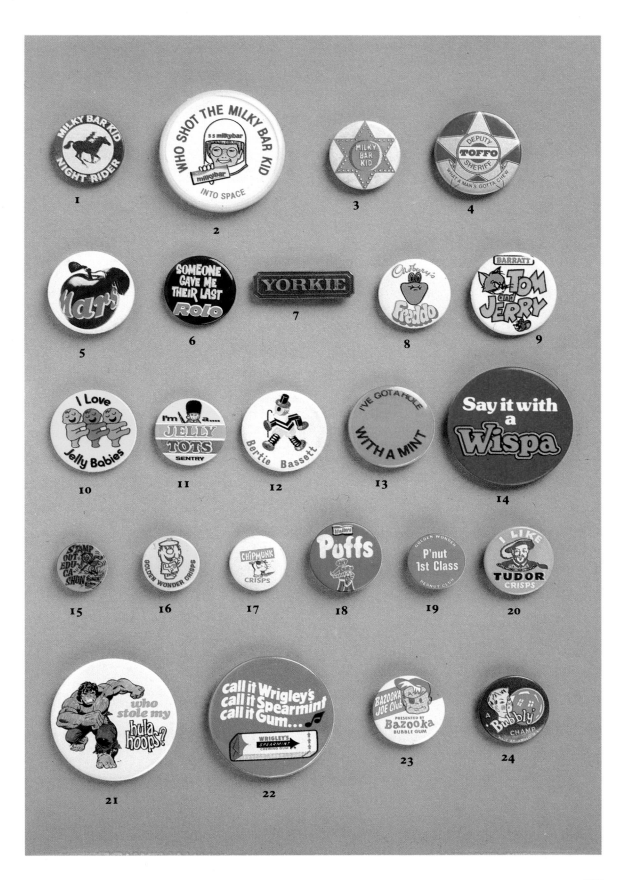

Ice cream

It was an Italian, Carlo Gatti, who started the practice of selling ice cream to the general public from barrows in London in the early years of this century. The ice cream vans we know today developed after the Second World War as techniques in refrigeration improved. Competition between rival firms heightened during the 1950s. One such firm was Rossis of Southend-on-Sea. Their 1 in (25 mm) design featured two pointed cornets and was made by Thomas Fattorini Ltd. It must be one of the oldest ice cream badges. Other companies, such as Mr Napoli and Tonis also feature on badges.

During the 1960s ice cream badges and ice creams themselves, were influenced by the space race. Lyons Maid, in particular, featured several space themes. Their 'Galaxy Patrol' set of the mid–1960s includes a space pilot, fleet colonel, attack leader (all $1\frac{1}{4}$ in/32 mm) and a commander-in-chief ($2\frac{1}{4}$ in/57 mm). Later designs showed Joe 90, a famous TV puppet star ($1\frac{1}{4}$ in/32 mm) and a rocket-shaped lolly, the 'Zoom' ($1\frac{1}{4}$ in/32 mm lithograph). Walls also had a rocket-shaped lollipop, 'Sky Ray' ($1\frac{1}{4}$ in/32 mm). Rossis had a space club with badges ($1\frac{1}{2}$ in/38 mm).

Mr Whippy, Mr Softee, and Lord Neilson also issued standard badges featuring their logo during the 1960s. Mr Softee has since issued several 1 in (25 mm) and $1\frac{1}{4}$ in (32 mm) designs (some lithographs); Miss Softee was introduced in the 1970s.

A popular ice cream theme of the 1960s was the Safety Club. So many children had been injured or killed running to or from ice cream vans that some sort of safety promotion was important. These include 'Walls Kerb Driller', 'Mr Softee says Safety First', 'Mr Whippy Safety Club', and 'Lyons Maid Mind How You Go'.

By 1967 the shaped lolly had well and truly arrived and, since then, a host of shapes have been produced. Lyons Maid promoted many of their lollies with lithographed $1\frac{1}{4}$ in (32 mm) badges. These include the 'Haunted House' set. Other lollies similarly promoted are Orange Dragon, Freak Out, Red Devil, Brrr Blobs, and Jelly Terror. Into the 1980s Dayvilles, boasting 32 different flavours, came to London with the idea of having a chain of outlets across Britain under the American system of franchising.

Matey Bubble Bath

Since Matey was launched in Britain in the mid-1960s they have issued several sets of badges as well as single badges during at least 12 promotional campaigns.

At least four sets, each comprising six designs, had been issued by 1985. These were normally given away stuck to the lid of the bottle. The sets include a prehistoric creatures set numbered one to six ($1\frac{3}{4}$ in/45 mm), a set of ships ($1\frac{3}{4}$ in/45 mm), and perhaps their best loved set of six whales 'Save the Whale with Matey and the World Wildlife Fund' ($2\frac{1}{8}$ in/55 mm). In 1982 a 'Matey around the World' set of six $2\frac{1}{4}$ in (57 mm) designs was issued: Red Indian, Dutch lady, alpine horn, camel and pyramids, Venetian gondolier and Eskimo. A 'Save the children' $2\frac{1}{8}$ in (55 mm) badge was also given away in 1982. Single designs issued include 'Matey Bubble Bath' $1\frac{3}{4}$ in (45 mm), and an early design (1969 to 1970) 'I'm a super matey shipmate', $1\frac{1}{2}$ in (38 mm).

Ice cream and bubble bath

1 to 11 Ice cream designs of the 1950s and 1960s. Apart from the safety theme (6), space is very dominant. 1 is a Thomas Fattorini Ltd design. 3 and 4 are lithographs. 9 and 10 are part of a set 12 to 18 Ice cream designs of the 1970s and 1980s. 12 to 15 and 17 are lithographs, 13 coming from a set of at least six 18 Dayvilles initial promotion included at least three badge designs
19 to 24 Matey Bubble Bath badges. 19 is an original 1960s design. 22 is from a set of six ships. 23 is from a lithographed set of six prehistoric creatures, mid-1970s. 24 is from a 1982 set of six 'Around the World' designs

The Robertson's golly

Early designs

A son of James Robertson discovered gollies, the little black rag dolls, during a visit to the United States before the First World War. His decision to use this as an emblem for his company was a fortuitous one indeed. The first brooch was introduced between 1920 and 1923, packaged between the then stone jar and the wrapping. These brooches are extremely rare and they were made of a bakelite substance with a pin fixture at the back.

A promotional campaign between 1924 and 1928 saw the introduction of a second golly brooch. This was made of painted tin with fabric used for long black hair. A loop on top of the head enabled it to be used as a pendant. These badges are also extremely rare.

The first enamel golly brooch was designed by H W Miller of Birmingham who approached Robertson's in 1928. The brooch was a golfer with a white waistcoat and downcast eyes and was given to the wife of James Robertson's salesman on 15 May, 1930. Robertson's liked the idea and a golly golfer and then a standard golly were produced. Both had black pupils in the centre of white eyes and yellow waistcoats with Golden Shred printed on top. These early enamels were given free on receipt of 10 paper gollies collected from Robertson's jars.

The scheme was a great success and in 1934 six golly fruit badges were produced by Miller. The fruit designs included the pop-eyed golly. Between 1937 and 1939 footballer and cricketer gollies were produced. Footballers had different coloured footballs, to represent most of the first division teams: red and white, blue and white, and black and white. The eyes of the footballers remained pop-eyed, but in 1938 the size of the pupils was increased.

Postwar designs

During the war years no gollies were made, and the original moulds were destroyed. In 1946 the scheme was relaunched using 10 new golly brooches, two fruit brooches and a small golly pendant. The yellow waistcoat became white and still had 'Golden Shred' on it. Pop-eyes remained on only four designs, the standard, footballer, cricketer, and boy scout, and also the pendant. The other designs—a golfer, skater, tennis player, hockey player, bagpiper and guitarist—had golly looking downwards. The two fruit badges were the lemon and the raspberry. Ten paper gollies still had to be collected to get these brooches, and these also were redesigned to a smaller size enabling them to fit under the cardboard lid in each jar of preserves.

The success of the scheme was such that 50,000 brooches per week were being issued from Robertson's factories in 1949. Millers couldn't cope with such large quantities and Fattorini and Sons helped out. When Millers ceased trading in the early 1960s other manufacturers were called in. The demand was such that Robertson's made it harder for consumers to qualify for a brooch. The paper gollies were reissued in 21 new sporting or musical designs. Ten different designs of paper golly were required to qualify for a brooch, and Robertson's promoted other flavoured preserves in this way.

The Robertson's golly

The golly brooches are perhaps the most collected of all the badges in this book and, since the 1970s, they also became among the most controversial.

1 to 3 County cricketers of 1937 to 1939 on presentation card. The cricketers were yellow-waistcoated and included the county name at the base of the brooch. At least 16 first-class county cricket clubs were available, as well as Australia and England teams.

4 One of six golly fruits of 1934 which included a golly head on the design

5 Prewar golly competitor. Several other producers of jams and marmalades issued enamel brooches. 'Sweet Nell' accompanied Nell Gwynne Marmalade in an attempt to take some trade from Robertson's Golden Shred, which had over 50 per cent of the marmalade market. The owners of Nell Gwynne, Crosbies Preserving Company were eventually bought out by Robertson's around 1965

6 A selection of the 21 postwar tokens to be collected from jars sent to Robertson's for brooches

7 to 20 Brooches from 1946 to 1968. After 1956 several manufacturers were used to make the brooches, and slight variations occur on certain gollies. Manufacturers of those shown are: H W Miller (*7, 9, 11*); Fattorini and Sons (*8, 10, 12, 13, 17, 20*); R E V Gomm (*14, 16, 18, 19*); J R Gaunt, London (*15*)

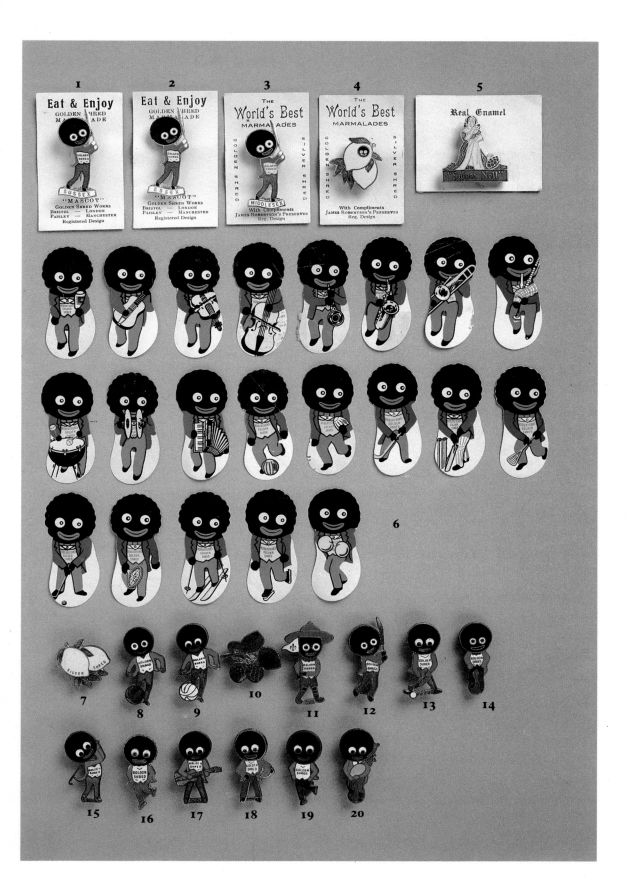

Modern gollies

Hermetically sealed jars with metal lids were introduced in 1956, making it no longer possible to put the paper golly under the lid. After initially being stuck to the top of the lid, they were eventually slipped behind the label. This practice continued until the early 1970s when the supermarket age meant that children could remove the golly tokens from the jars on the shelves, thus defeating the system. The result was the printing of the golly on the actual label, together with instructions on how to get the brooch.

Between 1956 and 1968 demand was so great that several manufacturers were used to help out with the making of the brooches. Apart from Miller and Fattorini and Sons these include: Toye, Kenning and Spencer; Firmin; Melsom Products; Graham Products; Davis Badges; Olympic; W O Lewis; and R E V Gomm. In 1968 the boy scout's hat was changed to a green beret, and a lollipop man was issued with Golden Shred printed on his coat.

In 1970 a completely new set was issued. These were made by R E V Gomm and have yellowy orange waistcoats with no writing and the hair is scalloped. A special golly balloon badge was made in 1974, and this is very scarce.

By 1981 acrylic gollies replaced the Gomm enamels, these 'new look' gollies being made in Taiwan. They are: commemorative golly with Union Jack waistcoat, cyclist, skier, fruits-strawberry, raspberry, orange, lemon and blackcurrant—footballer, standard golly pendant with legs astride and hands on hips. 1981 additions were: standard golly with left arm raised, golfer, bagpiper, tennis player, racing motorcyclist, cricketer, guitarist, and traffic warden. 1982 additions were: astronaut, policeman, nurse, baker, fireman, cowboy, doctor, Ali Jamjar (a bottle bank promotion), a sailor (HMS *Crichton*, the minesweeper, has a golly mascot and this badge is issued to crew members). 1985 additions were: fisherman, butcher and milkman, ambulanceman, postman, Canadian Mountie and Sailor.

Golly button badges

In the late 1950s early 1960s three 1 in (25 mm) button badges were issued. Two featured the standard golly, one on a white background and one on a red background. The other design was for Gollicrush, Robertson's orange drink. These were made by J R Gaunt of Birmingham. In 1976 four 1 in (25 mm) lithographs were produced, each featuring golly with the right arm raised and the words 'Golden Shred' around the perimeter. These come in four background colours—red, blue, yellow and white. In 1980 a Fifty Golden Years $2\frac{1}{8}$ in (55 mm) lithograph design was issued and, in 1984, a $2\frac{1}{2}$ in (64 mm) lithograph, 'I'm Golly! Buy me' was produced.

Variations

The period 1946 to 1969 produced many variations in the designs, simply because more manufacturers were involved. Serious collectors look for any minute difference, and it is part of the Badge Collectors Circle's aim to discover these. Moreover, certain special badges are rumoured to exist. It was rumoured that a Scottish kilted golly was produced, but this is as yet unproven. Similarly, the collectability of the golly is such that fakes or copies do exist. Most of those noted by 1985 concern the 1970s skier and motorcyclist.

The modern golly

1 to 14 A selection of R E V Gomm enamel gollies produced from 1970 to 1981. They have plain yellow waistcoats
15 to 23 Gollies from 1981—five fruits, skier, footballer, cyclist and commemorative golly. Some of these have a shiny plastic finish. It appears that during this period Robertson's were trying out new, cheaper, alternatives to the enamel brooch. The new-look brooches are made in Taiwan
26 to 33 Ultimately Robertson's settled for a non-shiny plastic surface on these 1982 to 1984 additions
24 and 25 Two counterfeit or bootleg gollies in unusual colours. These were on sale in gift shops in 1984, and are copies of *12* and *14*, the 1970 designs by R E V Gomm. Someone had obviously copied those 1970s badges in a variety of different colours. However, such is the demand for gollies that even the fakes are sought after
34 to 42 Various golly button badges 1950s to 1980. *34* was part of a set for Hintons Supermarket around 1976. *35* to *37* are 1950s designs. *38* and *39* are two of four mid-1970s badges, lithographs. *40* is one of the 'Get it in glass' set of the late 1970s that featured golly. *41* is a 1980 commemorative lithograph. *42* is a $2\frac{1}{2}$ in (64 mm) frying pan golly of the early 1980s

Christmas

Visiting Santa in his department-store grotto became a popular seasonal treat after the 1950s. Many of these Santas issue badges, advertising their store. Nearly all these are button badges and those of the 1950s and 1960s are normally 1 in (25 mm) or 1¼ in (32 mm), becoming bigger and more diverse in the 1970s. Some of the larger stores, such as Debenhams, are big enough to make lithographs viable, and 'We met at Debenhams' are among the most common Santa designs. Most badges say 'I've met Santa at . . . . . .', or words to that effect. Some designs relate to a toy fair at the shop in question, or simply say 'Happy Christmas from . . .'.

Manufacturers often produce standard Santa drawings, and fill in a different name on the design. Older badges tend to have better illustrated Santas; the designs since 1970 are often plainer and more of a cartoon nature. Other designs feature popular children's characters, such as 'Christmas with the Muppets at Selfridges' (1981). Selfridges have quite a tradition for Christmas badges and Uncle Holly is unique to them. Originating from before the First World War, Uncle Holly walks round the store and speaks to the children at Christmas time. In the 1950s and 1960s a 1 in (25 mm) badge, 'Member of the Uncle Holly Circle' was distributed.

Other Christmas badges include 'Order your Co-op Christmas hamper now', 1¼ in (45 mm) or 'The magical world of Chistmas City Centre Manchester right to the heart of things', 1½ in (38 mm), or 'Make someone happy phone your Christmas greetings Cardiff telephones', a 1¾ in (45 mm) design featuring Buzby.

Another trend developing in the 1980s is for preserved railway lines to boost their out-of-season business by running Santa specials. Several preserved lines run steam trains to Greenland or Santaland, and Santa either gets on the train to do his job or a station is suitably decked out. Badges commemorating such rides are proving more popular and add to the growing number in this category.

Another addition, since the 1970s badge boom, has been those sold in novelty and gift shops, and on Christmas cards. A set of five 2⅛ in (55 mm) lithographs, made in Hong Kong, includes 'Santa is brill', 'Snowmen are softies', 'Santa loves me', 'ILCP' (I like Christmas pudding), and 'IBGTY' (I've been good this year). Other 2⅛ in (55 mm) badges, such as 'Merry Christmas' and 'I believe in Father Christmas' are sold in novelty shops. Imports from Hong Kong include plastic mechanical badges, one of which has Santa popping out of a chimney when a string is pulled.

Anti-Christmas badges are not particularly common, but as commercialism gets crazier there is plenty of the 'I hate Christmas' feeling, and these badges could well become commoner. It does seem a pity that designs with the Nativity are almost non-existent, but Father Christmas does not have a total monopoly. The women's movement has inspired designs including 'Mother Christmas brings better presents', 1½ in (38 mm). Karl Marx also gets in on the act on a 'Happy Marxmas' badge. The Legalize Cannabis campaigners issued a clever design which looks like Christmas trees and snow with Merry Christmas, but is actually cannabis leaves, snow and 'Merry Wanna', 1¾ in (45 mm).

Badges are part of seasonal promotions.

1 to **11** Straightforward 'I've met Santa' designs: *1* and *3* are late 1950s badges; *2* is late 1970s White and Lambert; *4* and *5* are Debenhams' lithographs from the early 1980s. *7* is from a now defunct Sheffield store, White and Lambert 1977. *8* and *9* show the use of the same design; *10* is from 1983; *11* is a White and Lambert 1977

13 and **14** Preserved railway Santa specials from the early 1980s; *13* is from White and Lambert

15 A 1982 design promoting Christmas shopping in Manchester

16 Hong Kong lithograph given with greetings card, one of four designs

17 and **18** Selfridges Christmas badges—Muppets 1981, Uncle Holly 1967

19 to **21** Three of a set of 12 second-surface printed designs on a metal base of the early 1980s, more correctly described as brooches

22 to **24** Alternative designs. *22* is a take-off of the Anti-Nazi League design. *23* is a clever design complete with cannabis leaf symbol from the Legalize Cannabis campaign. *24* is a Mother Christmas badge from the women's movement in the early 1980s

25 Pop-up plastic Santa, 1984

Miscellaneous products

Paint

The first Dulux old English sheepdog appeared in 1964. His name was Dash and he was such a success that the scheme was continued with Digby, chosen in a special competition to be his successor. Digby retired in 1978 when Dillon took over, but to millions he is simply the Dulux dog, and he has appeared on countless badge designs, the most common being a set of $2\frac{1}{8}$ in (55 mm) lithographs.

Shoes

'Clark's Lucky Two-Shoe Club—league of foot freedom' is an enamel design complete with dangling shoes. The 'Lucky Two-Shoe club' began in the early 1950s and ended in 1968. A child, on receiving his or her first pair of shoes, was given a badge by the retailer. The retailer kept a record of the child's birthday and sent a birthday card each year. Apart from the 'Lucky Two-Shoe' register there were 'Lucky Two-Shoes musical chairs' for sitting on while feet were being measured. The comedian, Willie Rushton, wore his 'Lucky Two-Shoe' badge regularly on television. Clark's estimate that about 500 retailers conscientiously participated in the scheme.

Clark's Commandos began in 1969 to promote the shoes of that name. Badges were issued in association with a comic strip, Kit Carter, through the retailers. A coloured plug code in the base of the shoe indicated the shoe size, and the badge to be awarded. At least five different Commandos badges exist and, although the scheme ended in 1973, some retailers had stocks of badges which lasted until 1979 when the 'Commando' disappeared.

From 1979 to 1982 Clark's sponsored the London Whirligig Theatre. Apart from a standard 'Whirligig-Clark's' badge there is also a 'R U A nut case 2' design for the theatre's production of the *Nutcracker Suite* in 1980. In 1984 through Peter Lord shops and in time for the Olympics, they issued a set of $2\frac{1}{8}$ in (55 mm) designs, 'Fit feet', featuring different Olympic events.

Jeans

Wranglers, Levis, and Brutus have all issued badges several of which come in sets. In the late 1970s Wrangler adopted the mascot approach—if that's what Mr Wrangler can be called. Badges were given with new pairs of jeans. At least six different designs were issued, including: 'Mr Wrangler likes me', 'Mr Wrangler says to smile', and 'Good grief Wrangler'. Later badges showed a dog, Wralph Wrangler.

Levis issued a set of at least four $2\frac{1}{4}$ in (57 mm) designs, their slogan being 'Levis the leader of the pack'. Brutus issued at least seven different designs for their 'Brutus feels good' campaign. The Brutus set is lithographed and is in a pop art style. There are many other badges in this growing section.

Supermarkets and shopping centres

Since the opening of the first supermarkets in the 1960s hundreds of badges have been issued for the various big chains, as well as for smaller local supermarkets. The development in the 1970s of new shopping centres has also spawned badges. Spar supermarkets have

Other products

1 Clark's Lucky Two-Shoe Club enamel made by Fattorini and Sons Ltd, 1950s to 1968. The badge should have two miniature shoes dangling from the base
2 Clark's Commandos, lithograph 1969 to 1973. One of at least four similar designs
3 Clark's Commandos, also a lithograph
4 1984 'Fit feet' from an Olympics set of at least four designs made up by Baynham and Stanfield
5 From 1979 to 1982 Clarks sponsored the Whirligig Theatre. This badge was for a 1980 production of the *Nutcracker Suite*
6 'Brutus feels good', one of a set of at least seven lithographs, mid-1970s
7 A design given away with Wrangler jeans around 1979
8 One of a set of at least four designs from the early 1980s
9 Dynorod, the drain unblockers, issued an interesting set of badges in the early 1980s. The set of six designs made little sense individually but together formed a humorous comic strip, based on the Battle of Britain. Our daring pilot is the Dynorod leader and his plane is a Dynorod van. The enemy is a blocked toilet
10 One of several Top Shop designs of the late 1970s; this one was made up by White and Lambert
11 Lithograph of the Dulux dog, one of at least five colours from the late 1970s
12 Start-rite shoes, an early 1980s design by Lonsto of London
13, 14 and 20 Late 1960s badges from supermarkets. *13* is a 1 in (25 mm) lithograph
15 1979 Spar supermarket design, lithograph
16 1980 Spar promotion
18 Beaumont Leys Shopping Centre near Leicester opened in 1984. The badge made up by Baynham and Stanfield
19 One of many DIY supermarket designs of the early 1980s

been keen users of badges for their promotional campaigns. In the early 1970s they used Disney characters for their 'Disney on parade' promotion. Later they adopted 'Savings are just around the corner' in $1\frac{1}{2}$ in (38 mm) and $2\frac{1}{8}$ in (55 mm) lithographs, and their 'So near so far' slogan features on a set of at least four badges.

Food

The HP baked beans promotion of the early 1960s included a set of $1\frac{1}{4}$ in (32 mm) badges with racing car designs. The popular jingle, 'A million housewives every day pick up a tin of beans and say "Beanz meanz Heinz"' written by Johnny Johnson, inspired a campaign that encouraged young children to compose and recite poems about 'Beanz'. Of the scores of children who sent in poems few got on television, but most received a badge 'Heinz Beanz Bard'.

In 1967 Cadbury/Typhoo began marketing Smash instant mashed potato and a few years later the Smash martians appeared. 'For mash get Smash' was the jingle by Cliff Adams, another jingle wizard. These 42 in (102 cm) high metallic versions of the Brooke Bond chimps were an instant hit. They appear on a $1\frac{1}{2}$ in (38 mm) lithograph design, 'My Mum's a Smasher'.

Two campaigns which adopted the 'Rules OK' slogan were 'Spam Rules OK' and 'OK Sauce Rules OK'.

An interesting 1980 promotion by Princes Pastes included the conversion of the lid of the jar into a badge. Details on the side of the jar explained what to do, and on writing to Princes, a $2\frac{1}{4}$ in (57 mm) badge, 'I'm in the Prince's Badge Club', was sent, together with plastic clips for the lid badges. The lids featured cartoon creatures according to the flavour of the paste. Sammy and Sidney were fish pastes: Helga, Henrietta and Hilda were chicken flavour.

In the late 1970s the Meat Marketing Board set about promoting British meat. 'British Meat's got the lot' features on $1\frac{3}{4}$ in (45 mm) and $2\frac{1}{4}$ in (57 mm) badges in a variety of colours.

Beefeaters, Little Chefs, Wimpys and Kentucky Fried Chicken fast food outlets were sprouting up everywhere at the end of the 1970s. Many of these issued badges. The Wimpy chain adopted Mr Wimpy. From 1979 to 1985, at least seven sets were issued, usually with four or five designs in each. These sets include: sports, space, Pepsi, Coca Cola, Round the world, and a party set. Many of them are lithographed with solid backs, by Anterior. Beefeater Steakhouses adopted the Mr Men characters around 1980 and by 1985 there were well over twenty different designs. Burgerland issued a set with all of their different burgers and other dishes on, at least six in all. The 'Biggest fish and chip shop in the world', Harry Ramsden's at White Cross, Guiseley in Yorkshire, gave away a 2 in (50 mm) design, 'I'm just wild about Harry Ramsden's' in 1978. The clown Ronald McDonald was devised by McDonald's hamburgers in about 1982, and he features on some of their badge designs. Others include 'Keep your eyes on your fries', $2\frac{1}{8}$ in (55 mm).

Junk food had its detractors. 'I ate at a motoring services and lived', $1\frac{1}{4}$ in (32 mm) is a humorous thought on one badge, and 'Fresh is best' a more sober one.

Food

1 One of an early 1960s set of four from HP baked beans
2 and 3 Heinz Beans badges
4 Spam lithograph of late 1970s using that 'Rules OK' slogan
5 OK sauce also used 'Rules OK' in their early 1980s set of four
6 and 7 Princes' Badge Club of 1982 used the lids of their jars as badges (7). 6 was the club badge which came with fittings for the lids which were not very successful
8 British meat promotion. This design was issued in at least two sizes and two colours
9 Dewhurst Butcher's promotion of 1981
10 and 11 Examples of the various sets produced by Wimpy. There was a Coca-Cola set as well as a Pepsi. 11 was for the 1982 World Cup
12 One of a set of at least six for Burgerland in the early 1980s
13 Lithograph from Smash instant potatoes, late 1970s
14 A Westfield Advertising design made up by White and Lambert for a chip shop in Ballymena
15 One of a set of two, later followed by Roland McDonald designs in 1983
16 Little Chef standard design issued since 1978
17 and 19 Designs from the opponents of fast food
18 Harry Ramsden's in Yorkshire is 'the biggest chip shop in the world'
20 In 1981 Beefeater used the Mr Men on their badges and were still doing so in 1985. (Over 20 designs have been issued)

1

2

3

4

5

6

7

8

9

10

11

12

13

14

15

16

17

18

19

20

Services

Post office—British Telecom

In 1978 the postal authorities were concerned about losses on the parcels side of their business. A total of £45,000,000 was being lost annually. They adopted a marketing campaign aimed to attract more firms to send packets and small freight by post, for which reduced rates were offered. Postmen and others wore the badge 'We mean business', 2¼ in (57 mm). Similar campaigns include the promotion of the post code throughout the 1970s. Postmen and dogs do not always get on well together, and a public relations campaign issued 'I'm a postman's pal', 2¼ in (57 mm), in 1978.

One Post Office campaign stands out from the rest: Buzby! During the mid-1970s Buzby became such a popular character that by 1978 a set of at least 12 designs, showing Buzby in various guises, was on sale at gift shops and the like at 40p each. The 'Buzby Junior Club' complete with 1¾ in (45 mm) badge began. As with the Smurfs, people quickly became tired of Buzby's constant appearances.

Fuel

Coal, gas and electricity have all used badges as part of major promotional campaigns. Mr Therm, the gas mascot, had been used since the 1930s, the days of the Gas Light and Coke Company. He was sacked in 1962. An enamel badge featuring Mr Therm is popular with collectors of enamels. In the mid-1970s a new mascot in the shape of a blue flame, 'Mr Gas', was adopted and appears on various designs, notably 'Gas gets on with it'.

During the 1970s, saving energy was a major theme, and the Electricity Council issued badges such as 'The Medallion Award' or 'I'm an energy saver' for those who cut down. 'Economy 7' was being promoted at the same time as an energy saver, and the slogan 'Think electric' was adopted. This was later extended to 'Farm electric', 'Shop electric', 'Cook electric', and so on. An alternative design, prefixing 'Think electric' with 're' was a further indication of the search for alternative sources of energy.

The armed forces

Since 1960 the armed forces have encouraged recruitment by playing on the themes of patriotism and glamour. The navy have used several slogans, such as 'Fly Navy', 'Dive Navy', 'Sail Navy', or 'Everybody's somebody in the Royal Navy'. A counter to these designs is the badge, 'Join the army, meet interesting people and kill them', which has been issued in several sizes.

Building societies and banks

Since the mid-1970s there has been a dramatic growth in the number of building societies and the services they offer. Competition between rival companies has led to give-aways such as badges. Some of these badges are related to children's savings clubs and show a mascot of some sort. Others are straightforward logo badges or follow-ups from television campaigns.

1 to 4 Buzby was adopted by British Telecommunications, but by the time the company launched its share issue Buzby was dead. *1* is in moulded plastic. *2* is a standard design issued in millions. *3* is an alternative design. *4* was supplied by Hardisty Rolls of Harrogate
5 to 8 Other GPO designs. Postman Pat superseded Postcode Pete in 1983–4
9 to 11 Promotions for the armed forces and their alternative (*10*)
12, 15, 16, 18 to 20 Banks and building societies have produced hundreds of badges, especially from 1980 to 1985. *12* is a mid-1970s design and since that time the TSB have issued at least seven similar designs. *15* is the second-surface printed 'Busy Bee' of the Haywards Heath Building Society. *16* is moulded plastic *18*. The cartoon Access 'I'm your flexible friend' came from the Wyatt-Cattaneo combination that produced the flour graders and the Tetley tea folk. Access features on a 2¼ in (57 mm) badge.
13 and 14 Many 'Think Electric' designs were issued from 1977 to 1985. *14* is the alternative design
17 Mr Therm, an enamel design in use from the 1930s to 1962 when Mr Therm officially died

Places, holidays and leisure

At the turn of the century, those who could afford a holiday in one of the growing number of resorts around Britain, were able to choose from a variety of souvenirs to take home. Enamelled badges fixed to the ends of spoons or sides of letter racks were among them, as well as actual enamel badges.

In the 1930s many working people were granted holidays with pay for the first time. Souvenir shops began to flourish, although it wasn't until the 1950s that the sale of button badges in such shops became commonplace.

Many of the earlier button badges were used to advertise the holiday resort. In the late 1930s, Thomas Fattorini's catalogues show two such button badge designs: 'Oyez Oyez found a perfect holiday resort—Cliffsand Bay' and 'Barry—come where you can revel in sunshine'. Next to the Barry badge it states 'A casual remark about the badge has frequently been the reason for the wearer telling his friends of the amenities of the resort, resulting in another family spending a happy holiday there. We make thousands of these badges every year—is your resort represented?' Since of the thousands made few are to be found today, a prewar resort button badge is a treasure indeed.

Enamel badges continued to be made for places, and grew in popularity with button badges in the 1950s and 1960s. Although for every enamel made there must have been at least a thousand button badges, the older button badges are just as hard to find.

It was in the 1950s that button badges began to be issued in greater numbers. As the holiday industry developed so too did the souvenir shops. Often designs were duplicated on sew-on embroidered badges. C J Wood and Company of Bristol was one such company who produced thousands of place badges in the 1950s and early 1960s. C J Wood and Company is now defunct, believed to have stopped producing in the late 1960s. Their badges were nearly all 1 in (25 mm) button badges initially, with simple but attractive designs. It is interesting that the company's name appears on them, showing that they employed a middle man to go round the souvenir shops to get the trade.

From the 1950s onwards the market broadened to include zoos and stately homes. London was an obvious target for the badge makers and C J Wood and Company would send out cards to be displayed in shop windows stating, 'Local set of pin button badges—wear them and collect them'. Normally there were six in a set. Another C J Wood innovation in the 1960s was a plastic badge with a reflective insert, and the maker's name applied to the rear of the insert.

From 1975 onwards there was a steep decline in seaside badges but a general increase in those for museums, zoos and wildlife parks. This chapter is mainly arranged by manufacturer; other categories include cruises, holiday camps and hostels.

Place badges

Always popular as souvenirs, place badges illustrate the changing British holiday, from seaside jaunts to modern theme parks.
1 to **6** London shop display card issued by C J Wood and Company, Frenchay, Bristol, in the 1950s
7 and **8** Place enamels. 7 is by W O Lewis (Badges) Ltd, Birmingham
9 and **10** Badges for working men's outings of the 1950s
11 An early Mablethorpe design made up by White and Lambert
12 This C J Wood and Company design of the late 1960s never really caught on
13 to **29** A thematic collection from 1945 to 1985. *13, 15* and *17* were supplied by F W Hannah, Pershore. *14, 16, 18, 21, 22, 24, 25, 27, 28* and *29* were all made up by White and Lambert. *19* and *23* are by Jemah Products (Novelties) Ltd, Newton Abbott

Place badge manufacturers

Jemah

Jemah Products (Novelties) of Torquay began in 1960, a time when the seaside badge was at its zenith. They produced millions of other badges for the trade, but only applied their name to the holiday badges, for which they had their own artists. The artwork on their designs is very distinctive. The artwork was often taken from postcards. Over the 15 years of Jemah's existence there were probably about 10 artists working for them. Standard designs included local views, town crests or shields, beach scenes, and local curiosities.

The company moved from Torquay to Newton Abbot around 1963 and the address on the curl of the badge was altered accordingly. Their place designs were all 1 in (25 mm) and $1\frac{1}{4}$ in (32 mm) button badges, although their other badges were produced in sizes from $\frac{5}{8}$ in (12 mm) right up to 6 in (156 mm). They covered the country from John O'Groats to Land's End, and designs include those for zoos, amusement parks, and safari parks as well as seaside towns. One badge, for Exmouth Aquarium, is interesting because the place no longer exists. No doubt there are others like this.

Jemah also exported to countries all over the world. As well as button badges they also produced enamels, which did not bear the company name and were electroplated nickel silver with enamel on top. These enamels were usually heraldic shaped and about $\frac{1}{2}$ in (12 mm) across.

In 1975 Jemah went bankrupt and was taken over by Kildsware who continued to produce place badges. By the mid-1970s however, the market for souvenir badges of resorts had declined. Children were not so keen to show they had been to Blackpool or Eastbourne especially when they had probably been to more exotic places like Spain or the Canary Islands. However, places such as museums and country parks were still good for trade. In the 1980s for example, Kents Caverns have a set of four designs by Kildsware and turn over 20,000 of these a season.

White and Lambert crimped badges

White and Lambert's crimped place badges are normally either 1 in (25 mm), $1\frac{1}{4}$ in (32 mm) or $1\frac{1}{2}$ in (38 mm) button badges. The use of strong colours gives them a distinctive look. Often a design was issued for a number of different places, with perhaps a few slight changes here or there. The surfer is a common theme, and often crops up for different surfing resorts. Other designs issued for the same place also show slight variations, for example, there are at least four different versions of the St Michael's Mount badge. The badges all have the same design, but the writing varies as do the colours.

During the 1970s White and Lambert produced thousands of place badges, and would have dozens of designs for the same area, of which shops would often stock a variety. Badges were even produced for unlikely towns. Loughborough, for example, is not famous for attracting tourists, yet a local shopkeeper was persuaded to stock 1,000 badges which he duly sold for 10p each.

1 to **4** 1950s place designs of C J Wood and Company, Frenchay, Bristol. Their style was clearly imitated by Jemah Products
5 Electroplated nickel silver enamelled badge believed to have been supplied by Jemah
6 A design from the Taw Valley Company of Ilfracombe
7 to **45** Jemah Products (Novelties) Ltd, first of Torquay and then of Newton Abbott, was the most successful supplier of place badges from 1960 to 1975. The 1 in (25 mm) designs generally predate the $1\frac{1}{4}$ in (32 mm) which became popular later. *7* shows the Exmouth Aquarium, which had disappeared by 1984. *14* is an unusual royal badge from the Prince of Wales' Investiture, 1969. *17* and *18* show the use of the same design for different zoos. *26* and *39* are similar designs for different seaside resorts
46 Kildsware was the manufacturer that succeeded Jemah but by the late 1970s the demand for this type of badge was not so great

These distinctive designs made by White and Lambert disappeared around 1983, but the company made up many other place designs for other customers until they were taken over by W O Lewis in 1985. After this date they continued to produce button badges.

One of their customers was a shopkeeper in York. He bought White and Lambert coloured blanks, normally sold for school use, and glued his own print onto the blank, lacquering over the top. The tourists visiting York could purchase these 1¼ in (32 mm) designs for 10p each, featuring the Minster, the Shambles, and even Guy Fawkes who was born in York in 1570.

F W Hannah of Evesham

Hannah has supplied badges since 1970 and was still doing so in 1985. They are mostly 1¼ in (32 mm), 1½ in (38 mm) or 1¾ in (45 mm) button badges. Since the mid-1970s a plastic ring has been favoured. The name is applied on the curl, making them easily identifiable. One of the company's most notable customers is London Zoo. They sell at least 50,000 a year of this badge alone.

Colourmaster

Colourmaster (Photo Precision Ltd) are perhaps better known for postcard production, but around 1976 they decided to enter the badge market. On nearly all of their designs they use actual photographs, often taken from postcards. They work in 1½ in (38 mm) and 2⅛ in (55 mm) sizes, and code their designs on the curl. Originally badges were coded according to the place for which they were issued. One Beaumaris design is coded BLB9—Badge location B number 9—and any other places that began with B were in the same group. Around 1981 this system was changed. All 1½ in (38 mm) badges were coded BS, which could mean 'badge small'. By 1984 they had reached BS1000. Similarly, the 2⅛ in (55 mm) designs were recoded uniformly in 1981 to BX; by 1983 they had reached well over BX1100.

English Life

English Life, a Derbyshire concern, began producing badges in the early 1970s on a small basis. The prints were made up by White and Lambert. The vast majority of their designs are for museums, castles, and stately homes, a good indication of how the market had altered since 1960.

By 1985 English Life had at least 400 designs which were produced in lots of between 1,000 and 5,000. Prints are now made up by the London Emblem Company, and the name is on the back, meaning they are easily identifiable. The majority of their badges are 1½ in (40 mm) but they do issue some at 2⅛ in (55 mm) as well.

Place badge manufacturers

1 to **14** 1¼ in (32 mm) and 1½ in (38 mm) designs made up by White and Lambert from the late 1960s to the 1980s. Designs were often similar, such as the surfers (*6, 7* and *10*). Many slight variations exist (*1* to *3*). *11* is a 1983 variety made up for Amalco. Some 1970s examples have a small w on the curl, which could stand for Westfield, whose button badges are made up by White and Lambert
15 A White and Lambert yellow blank with a design glued on top and lacquered by a shopkeeper in York
16 to **20** Designs supplied by F W Hannah Ltd, originally of Evesham, from the early 1970s onwards
21 to **25** Colourmaster designs for 1976 to 1984, most of which were photographic, taken from their postcards. All designs were coded
26 to **30** English Life designs of the 1980s, made up by London Emblem Company

Other place badges

Enamel place badges are not uncommon. Certain designs are particularly popular, such as badges in the shape of lucky horse shoes.

Since the mid-1970s the London Emblem Company have produced many place badges, particularly for the big London museums. The Science Museum and the Natural History Museum have many designs featuring popular exhibits such as dinosaurs.

In December 1980 the British Museum commissioned three badges made with the slogan 'I have been to the British Museum' translated into three languages—classical Greek, Egyptian hieroglyphics, and Cuneiform. Unfortunately, the English proved to be a problem— 'Cuneiform' was misspelled 'Cunieform', and the whole batch of badges was withdrawn.

Skipton Castle has had a new button badge design every year since the early 1970s. If you multiply this by the number of tourist spots it gives you an idea of the scope of place badges. In the mid-1970s a reaction, not only to the number of badges, but also the number of tourists in certain places, gave rise to the slogan 'I am not a tourist, I live here'. This was produced in a variety of forms including a 'Smily face' version.

Fairly common since the late 1970s are badges with a metal disc backing into which is put a clear plastic disc printed with the design. The printing is usually in gold. London tourist attractions such as St Paul's Cathedral, and HMS *Belfast* have sold many thousands of these. One variation on this theme has a clear plastic surface inserted into a button-badge type back.

Circular, $1\frac{1}{4}$ in (32 mm) diameter, leatherette has been used also, in 2 mm thickness. This is often printed with gold foil on top of backgrounds of various colours. Moulded plastic badges of all sorts and shapes are also not uncommon.

Modern place badges

Today badges are more commonly issued for particular exhibitions, museums and amusement parks.
1 Skipton Castle issue a new design every year (White and Lambert)
2 The Arran design of 1982 shows the heart first used on 'I love New York' designs
3 and **4** Examples of the Smily face. *3* is a common slogan of the late 1970s
5 Gold-foiled leatherette badge of late 1970s, one of many produced for tourist attractions
6 Second-surface printed design inserted in a formed metal back around 1980
7 From the British Genius Exhibition in London in 1977
8 Kitchener appears in 1985 as well as on some of the very first button badges made during the Boer War
9 A badge for the Viking Exhibition at the British Museum, 1978–9
10 1985 design for a leisure park
11 West Country Marketing and Advertising design of 1984, one of many similar designs
12 One of many Natural History Museum dinosaur badges. This one is part of a London Emblem Company set from 1982
13 Enamel product by Stratton of Birmingham for the 1938 Empire Exhibition
14 1951 Festival of Britain logo reproduced in 1981 for some sort of commemoration. One of the original 1951 designs was in shaped plastic
15 Second-surface printed insert into a metal base
16 Skegness was still using John Hassall's 1908 Jolly Fisherman design in 1983
17 One of many similar moulded plastics—paint-filled by Westfield Advertising
18 Shaped plastic for the Liverpool Garden Festival
19 1983 London Emblem Company design for the Natural History Museum
20 and **21** *21* is the wrongly spelt version made for the British Museum in December 1980
22 1984 Cabinet War Rooms design featuring Churchill
23 Baynham and Stanfield in conjunction with Taylorscope produced a set of London badges for tourists in the late 1970s

1 — SKIPTON CASTLE YORKSHIRE
2 — I ♥ ARRAN
3 — I AM NOT A TOURIST I LIVE HERE
4 — I'VE BEEN TO COTSWOLD WILD LIFE PARK
5 — CORFE CASTLE
6 — HMS BELFAST
7 — I'm a BRITISH GENIUS
8 — IMPERIAL WAR MUSEUM WANTS YOU
9 — I've invaded the British Museum
10 — I DARED RIDE THE COBRA THE MEANEST RIDE IN EUROPE·WEST MIDLAND SAFARI & LEISURE PARK
11 — CURTIS MUSEUM & ALLEN GALLERY
12 — Natural History Museum DILOPHOSAURUS
13
14 — 1951
15 — JERSEY CHANNEL ISLANDS
16 — SUPER Skeggy
17 — WATCHET MARKET HOUSE MUSEUM
18 — International Garden Festival LIVERPOOL '84 2nd May to 14th October
19 — MAN'S PLACE IN EVOLUTION MODERN MAN NATURAL HISTORY MUSEUM
20 — I have been to the BRITISH MUSEUM CUNEIFORM
21 — I have been to the BRITISH MUSEUM CUNIEFORM
22 — CABINET WAR ROOMS
23 — ICH WAR HIER Piccadilly Circus, London

129

Butlin's

'Holidays with pay—Holidays with play. A week's holiday for a week's wage.' This was the slogan in Butlin's brochures in 1938. In that year Billy Butlin opened a new camp at Clacton, and invited all the Members of Parliament who had voted for the 'Holidays with Pay' scheme to the ceremony. The new legislation had undoubtedly ensured the huge success of Butlin's.

Two years earlier, in the spring of 1936, the first Butlin camp had opened at Skegness. It housed 1,000 people in rows of chalets, and the key to its attraction was that whatever the weather people could enjoy themselves. The idea for camp badges could well have come when Billy Butlin visited Cunningham's Young Men's Holiday Camp, a tent site on the Isle of Man. Butlin wanted to see large-scale catering in operation. While he was there he noticed campers wearing enamel badges with the Cunningham insignia. These badges identified who were bona fide camp visitors. In 1936, when Freda Monk of Nottingham arrived at Skegness as Butlin's first-ever camper, she was given a badge. Since then it is estimated that at least 1,750 different badges have been made for the Butlin organization. These can be categorized in two sections—camp badges and special badges.

Camp badges

Badges were issued at the following Butlin camps and hotels for the dates shown: Skegness, 1936 to 1939, and 1946 to 1967; Clacton 1938, 1939 and 1946 to 1967; Filey, 1945 to 1967; Pwllheli, 1947 to 1967; Ayr, 1947 to 1967; Mosney, 1948 to 1967; Brighton, 1953 to 1967; Blackpool, 1955 to 1967; Margate, 1955 to 1967; Bognor, 1960 to 1967; Minehead, 1962 to 1967; Barry, 1965 to 1967.

From 1948, variations in either colour or design occur so that more than one badge per camp per year was issued. For example, in 1955 there were three designs for Skegness. The prewar badges are quite scarce and sought after, and they were nearly all made by Thomas Fattorini. After 1945 a number of the big manufacturers were used and yet, strangely, not Thomas Fattorini. The prewar Skegness designs use the famous 'Jolly Fisherman' created by John Hassall, under the slogan 'Skegness is so bracing'—originally commissioned by the Great Northern Railway in 1908.

The Filey camp was built in 1939, but the war prevented it from opening until 1945. During the war, along with Clacton and Skegness, it was taken over by the government for military purposes. After the war the camps were sold back to Butlins for three-fifths of their original cost. Filey was opened for a few weeks in 1945 and their 'V for Victory Filey 1945' design is very scarce.

From 1946 to 1967 a great variety of interesting designs were produced for the various camps. Some have a local emblem, such as a thistle on the Ayr 1964 design, or the stags of Exmoor on the 1965 Minehead design. Others have a seaside flavour and a variety of bikini-clad ladies, buckets and spades, suitcases, and even crabs appear. In 1962 over a million people stayed at Butlin's, indicating the large number of badges that must have been made. The season of 1949 is said to have been bad for Butlin's and badges for that year are rarer.

Butlin's

These Butlin's Holiday Camp badges (1938 to 1959) illustrate the great variety in designs used. *1* is the Skegness design for 1938 and *4* is the Filey 1946 button badge. Known manufacturers are: Thomas Fattorini Ltd (*1*); Reeves and Company, Birmingham (*6, 7, 10, 12, 16, 31, 35*); Birmingham Medal and Badge Company (*8, 9*); Firmin, London (*13*); Jewellery Company, Dublin (*17, 19, 22, 23, 24, 28, 29, 30*); Fattorini and Sons (*21, 26*); J R Gaunt, London (*32, 33, 36*).

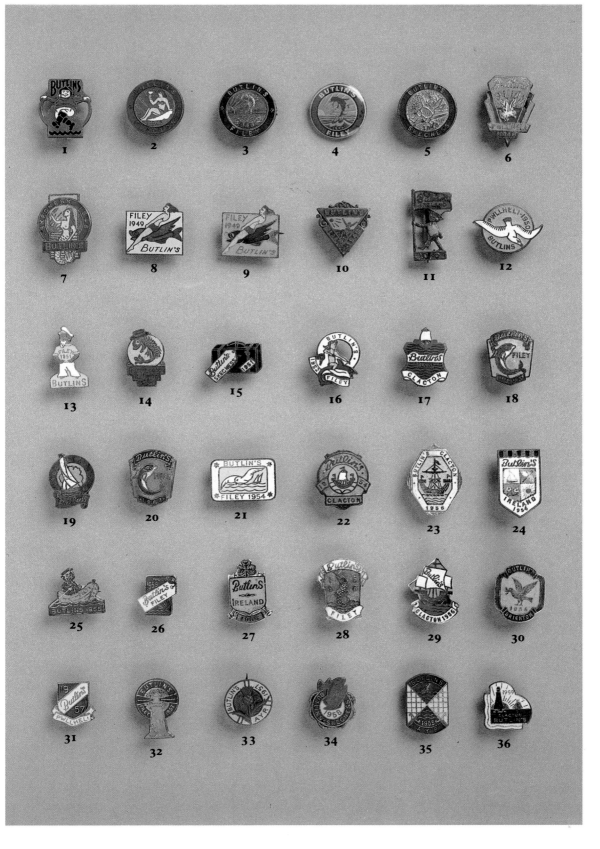

Special Butlin's badges

Butlin's second week

To indicate that you were on the second week of your holiday you were given a second week badge. There are at least nine different designs.

Butlin's staff badges

Early staff badges were the same shape and design as the annual camp badges. By 1950, separate designs were adopted, and ultimately there were 17 different shapes, each issued in three colours. The colours indicated the numbers of seasons worked: blue was for the first season, red for the second, and white for the third. From their fourth season onwards the staff wore a rectangular badge, which included the year that they started with Butlin's. The badges were numbered on the back and had to be handed in when the member of staff left. Head office staff wore designs with a Butlin's 'B' in the centre. Other variations are known. For the staff at Mosney, the Irish camp, the badge was a shamrock design with 'Staff' printed in the centre.

Beaver Club badges

Sir Billy Butlin, as he later became, worked alongside Lord Beaverbrook at the Ministry of Supply during the Second World War. It may only be coincidence that in 1951 the Butlin's club for 12-year-olds and under was called the 'Beaver', but many believe it was named after Lord Beaverbrook.

By 1961 there were 200,000 Beavers, and as well as Beaver annuals, Beaver money boxes, specially commissioned Beaver books (such as *Billy Bunter at Butlin's*), there were Beaver badges. Over the years several standard Beaver badges were issued. Beaver Club badges continued to be issued through the 1970s and 1980s, mostly printed discs put into a moulded metal back, not real enamels. In 1976 a '913' club was launched for 9- to 13-year-olds, as well as '15', a club for 15-year-olds.

Other Butlin's badges

The Royal Albert Hall Butlin's Festival of Reunion badges are of great interest. There were at least 10 reunions, including Beaver reunions and they all issued badges.

Butlin's issued a variety of special designs in addition to their camp badges.

1 to **26** Butlin's camp badges from 1960 to 1967. Known manufacturers are: W Reeves and Company, Birmingham (*1, 3, 4, 5, 12, 13, 16, 23, 26*); J R Gaunt, London (*2, 7, 11, 14, 17, 18*); Fattorini and Son, Birmingham (*6, 8, 9, 10, 22, 24*); Morton T Colver, Birmingham (*15, 19, 20, 21, 25*).

27 to **29** Second-week designs, of which at least nine different versions exist. Manufacturers are: Birmingham Medal and Badge Company (*27*); Firmin, London (*28*); J R Gaunt, London (*29*).

30 Button badge for honorary club member around 1950

31 One of at least 10 reunion badges

32 Filey committee design, by Jewellery Company, Dublin

33 Social club design, 1948–9

34 to **37** Beaver Club designs. *34* is a 1950s Beaver Club design by J R Gaunt, London. Four variations of this exist. *35* was used after *34* was discontinued in the early 1960s. *37* is one of at least six dated Beaver badges (J R Gaunt of London)

38 A painted insert design for the 913 Club, which was launched in 1976

39 1980s promotional button badges

40 1985 design for Butlin's Hotels Adventure Club

Other holiday camps and amusement parks

After the red coats of Butlin's the blue coats of Pontin's are perhaps best known. Sir Fred Pontin opened his first camp at Brean Sands, in 1947, near Weston-super-Mare on the site of a former military camp. There followed the opening of well over 20 camps, and many of these issued badges.

Middleton Tower, the Morecambe camp, issued year badges from at least 1952 to 1966, these being button badges. The Middleton Tower camp, also referred to as the Morecambe Bay Holiday Camp, ran children's clubs. The team names used for competitions were 'Saints' and 'Sinners'. Squires Gate, the Blackpool camp, also issued year badges and had a 'Junior Buccaneer's Club' complete with badge.

It is not always easy to determine Pontin's button badges as often only the name of the camp appears on the badge. Prestatyn Holiday Camp is one such example. Furthermore, during the 1960s within different camps different children's clubs existed. Later, standard button badges of various designs were issued and, by 1984, the 'Crocodile Club' was the children's club in all camps.

Warner's Holidays opened several camps in the 1950s. Their slogan, 'I'm on a Warner holiday', appears on standard issues for each year. The Warner's children's club was the Wagtails. This thrived in the 1950s and 1960s, and some $1\frac{1}{4}$ in (32 mm) year badges were issued as well as a variety of 1 in (25 mm) designs, all featuring the wagtail.

The Caravan Club and Camping Club have issued enamel badges to members, and many other holiday camps, parks and clubs have used button badges over the years. Many of the camps have since disappeared. Many caravan parks, too, have issued badges.

Amusement parks developed rapidly through the 1950s and 1960s, and by the 1980s the mass draw of sites like Alton Towers, Lightwater Valley, Britannia Park, West Midland Safari and Leisure Park and Blackpool Pleasure Beach were perfect outlets for thousands of badges.

The development of some of these sites is reflected in their badges. An Alton Towers badge from the late 1950s shows the house framed by a tree with no hint of what was to come.

In the 1970s and 1980s Ladbroke's Holidays 'Seagull Fun Club' issued a variety of designs usually featuring a cartoon seagull. A standard design was a shaped plastic Starcruiser badge in red and blue. Holiday Inn also started a children's club, 'The Johnny Holiday Club', in the early 1980s. Another 1980s' example is the 'Thomson Big T Club' badge.

Other camps and amusement parks

1 to 10 Pontin's Holiday Camp badges. Middleton Tower is near Morecambe. Squires Gate is the Blackpool camp. 7 and 8 were for teams at the Morecambe camp. 9 and 10 are late 1970s designs (8 and 10 are by White and Lambert)
11 and 12 Both badges made by Gaunt for clubs at the DMHC, Skegness, which was probably the Derbyshire Miners Holiday Club
13 to 16 Warner's camp and club badges
17 to 20 A variety of other camps and parks. 20 is a 1950s design
21 An enamel of the Camping Club of Great Britain and Northern Ireland, founded in 1901
22 to 26 A variety of badges for 1980s camps, clubs and amusement parks. 22 is shaped moulded plastic, foil-tipped. 26 is White and Lambert

1

2

3

4

5

6

7

8

9

10

11

12

13

14

15

16

17

18

19

20

21

22

23

24

25

26

Cruises

During the educational cruises of the SS *Nevada*, SS *Uganda*, and the MS *Devonian*, thousands of badges were issued to children to indicate their muster station and their 'house'. These were $1\frac{1}{4}$ in (32 mm) designs not unlike the 1 in (25 mm) school badges. They were mostly named after famous explorers—Columbus, Hunt, Rhodes, Younghusband, Chichester, Bell, Flinders, Grenfell, Stanhope and Howe. Enamel badges were also issued, some bearing the ship's flag, and others in the shape of the ship.

Sealink Ferries have also issued enamel badges of their fleet, and these 'ship shape' designs are very attractive. The Maritime Trust have issued $1\frac{1}{4}$ in (32 mm) button badges for their various exhibits, such as the 'Cutty Sark Greenwich', 'Gipsy Moth V Greenwich', and Herring Drifter Lydia Eva, Great Yarmouth'.

The pleasure boats of Scarborough and Bridlington have their own badges. It is not known when this practice started, but it probably reached its peak in the 1960s. The ships included: *Bridlington, Boys' Own, Mr Thornwick, Flamborian, TSS Yorkshireman, Yorkshire Belle, Bridlington Queen, Scarborough Coronia, Yorkshire Cruises, Regal Lady Cruises,* and the *Hispaniola*. In 1974 the *Hispaniola* issued a Jubilee Year badge 1949–74. *Scillonian III* of the Isles of Scilly, and the *Duke of Kent*, Eastbourne are two of many more such cruise boats that issued badges. Other boats are more static holiday attractions for example *SS Great Britain*, HMS *Victory* and HMS *Discovery*.

Youth hostels

The youth hostel movement owes much to Richard Schirrman, a German, who was appalled at the conditions which city children suffered and was prompted to provide healthy holidays in the country for them. At first he used school accommodation, but by 1909 the first hostel opened in Berg Altenon, Germany. During the 1930s, the idea spread to many neighbouring countries, including Britain. In 1930 the Youth Hostels' Association of Great Britain was formed, which later became the Youth Hostels Association (England and Wales) (YHA) when the Scottish Youth Hostels Association was formed (SYHA). Similar arrangements were made in Northern Ireland (YHANI) and also Eire (An Oige).

The aims of the YHA are 'to help all, especially young people of limited means, to a greater knowledge, love and care of the countryside, particularly by providing simple accommodation for them on their travels'.

The popularity of youth hostel badges developed between 1950 and 1970. Wearing a badge on your hat to show the hostels you had visited became popular. The great majority of hostel badges are 1 in (25 mm) button badges, often featuring beautifully drawn black-and-white pen-and-ink designs. Since 1970 $1\frac{1}{4}$ in (32 mm) designs became more commonplace and later there were $1\frac{1}{2}$ in (38 mm), $1\frac{3}{4}$ in (45 mm) and $2\frac{1}{8}$ in (55 mm) badges.

Apart from actual hostel badges there exist the official logo association badges, many of which are metal or enamel. Other YHA or SYHA badges include promotions, such as a $2\frac{1}{4}$ in (57 mm) 'Breakaway with SYHA' or celebrations such as 'YHA Golden Jubilee 1930 to 1980', $1\frac{3}{4}$ in (45 mm).

Pleasure cruises and youth hostels

1 to 18 A variety of badges for cruises and boating attractions from 1945 to 1985. Most of the Yorkshire badges are from the 1950s and 1960s. *8, 10* and *17* are by White and Lambert. *11* is by Colourmaster. *13* to *15* are from various educational cruises. *16* is a Fattorini and Sons enamel for educational cruises. *18* is one of two badges rushed out when the Athina B was grounded on Brighton beach and became a massive tourist attraction

19 to 35 A variety of Youth Hostel badges from 1945 to 1985. *19* and *22* are promotional designs of the late 1970s. *20* and *20a* are paint-filled standard designs by W O Lewis (Badges) Ltd. *21* is an enamelled design for the Scottish Youth Hostel Association (Badges Plus). *23* to *29* are 1 in (25 mm) black and white Youth Hostel classics produced from the 1950s onwards, but becoming rarer in the 1970s. *27, 28, 30* and *32* are by White and Lambert. *33* and *34* are larger hostel badges which became more popular from the late 1970s onwards

1   2   3   4   5   6

7   8   9   10   11

12   13   14   15   16   17

18   19   20   20   21   22

23   24   25   26   27   28   29

30   31   32   33   34   35

The media,

the famous and the fashionable

Prewar newspaper children's clubs

A whole galaxy of children's clubs in written publications have come and gone since the 1920s. For most of them a small fee is required to join and members are usually given a badge and membership card. Often there is a secret club code and the possibility of entering competitions or similar activities.

Newspaper clubs

Newspaper clubs for children developed very rapidly between 1919 and 1939 in the national dailies. Local newspapers soon followed their lead and since the 1920s there have been hundreds of such clubs, each issuing their own badge, including many classic enamelled badges.

One popular example is the *Daily Mirror* club, 'The Wilfredan League of Gugnuncs', WLOG. This was a 1920s club featuring a strip cartoon with characters such as Pip the dog, Squeak the penguin and Wilfred the rabbit. Auntie was an ancient bedraggled penguin and Popski an Eastern European villain who went around planting bombs. The secret greeting from one Gugnunc to another was 'Ick ick par boo' to which the answer was 'Goo goo par nunc'. The *Pip Squeak and Wilfred Annual* appeared each Christmas. The standard WLOG badge was a blue enamelled design. It depicted the elongated ears of a rabbit with the letters WLOG. The Wilfredan League of Gugnuncs is a typical example of the children's clubs of that time, and their popularity is underlined by the appearance in Thomas Fattorini's catalogue of 1939 of a whole page devoted to children's corner badges.

Other famous clubs of that time included the *Daily Express* Rupert League, the *Daily Mail* Teddy Tail League, the *Daily Herald* Bobby Bear Club, and the *Daily Record* Chum Club.

As well as the national newspapers, many local newspapers followed the trend. Most of these clubs were just children's corners, but sometimes they would adopt a mysterious title, such as the Leicester Mercury Oozoos Club. The Oozoos Club was a daily children's column which ran from 1925 to the outbreak of war in 1939. The column was conducted by Auntie Susie, (Mrs Winifred Goddard) and the main characters included Winky, Bobs, and Percy. The motto of the Oozoos was to 'be kind to animals'. There were well over 60,000 members in the 1930s, each having a badge and membership card.

The *Bradford Telegraph and Argus* Nig Nog Club was one of a number of Nig Nog clubs. Most of their badges were enamel, but one 'BT and A Nig Nog Club' badge is an interesting $\frac{3}{4}$ in (20 mm) button with a solid back and safety-pin fixing. Today the phrase 'Nig Nog' is highly offensive, but many of these old children's clubs adopted titles and mascots with such connotations. The *Bootle Times*, for example, features a golliwog on its 1 in (25 mm) children's corner badge of the early postwar period. Many local newspapers also had a 'Newshounds Club' which was popular with their young readers.

Children's corners

The fact that Thomas Fattorini Ltd devoted a whole page of their 1939 catalogue to children's corner badges indicates the high numbers produced. The Wilfredan League of Gugnuncs, WLOG, a design featuring rabbit ears is one of the best known, along with that for the Teddy Tail League.

CHILDREN'S CORNER BADGES

Get the children interested in your paper whilst they are young.
You will then have readers for life.

Have Badges which will do credit to your paper—Ask Thomas Fattorini Ltd. for a design and quotation.

Every child likes to belong to a Society and possess its Badge. This is why Children's Corners in Newspapers and Weekly Periodicals are so popular. One child has a Badge and shows it to its playmate who immediately wants one. If sent to subscribers or in return for coupons see how your circulation increases. Badges do increase circulation.

Most of our National Daily Newspapers and Weekly Journals have a Children's Corner and use Badges.

THOMAS FATTORINI LTD. REGENT STREET WORKS BIRMINGHAM, 1

PLEASE NOTE THE **THOMAS** IN OUR NAME AS SIMILAR FIRMS ARE **NOT** THE SAME

Postwar newspaper children's clubs

Since 1945 several national newspaper clubs have appeared. The Chipper Club of the early 1960s was run by the *Daily Mail* and *Evening Mail and Despatch*. The 1 in (25 mm) design featuring Chipper, a smiling dog, in the centre was made in a variety of colours. The *Daily Sketch* 'Pets' Police' has a badge, 'Pets' Cop', encouraging children to look after their pets. In 1959 Bruce Forsyth was used to promote them on a television commercial.

One of the most successful of the postwar clubs was the 'I Spy' Club. Initially run through the *News Chronicle* and *Daily Despatch* in the 1950s, children could join the great tribe of redskins and decode secret messages. A 1 in (25 mm) button badge 'I Spy Tribe' was issued. Later, in 1961, the *Daily Mail* took over and the badge just featured the 'I Spy' logo. There are slight variations in some of them. The highly successful *I Spy* books for children grew alongside the club.

In 1967 the *Observer* magazine issued a 'Watchdog' badge to keen-eyed readers of the *Young Observer*. The *Daily Mirror* began its Pop Club in the mid-1970s, and this later became the Rock and Pop Club. The *Mirror* also issued a badge to its *Junior Mirror* readers in 1981, a $2\frac{1}{4}$ in (57 mm) button badge.

Women's Realm 'Seekers Club' for 7- to 14-year-olds and 'Junior Seekers' Club for the under 7-year-olds, issued members with a badge and a membership card containing a Seekers secret code. Each week the magazine published a secret message, which when decoded was a quiz question. When 12 questions had been answered correctly, members were promoted to Seeker Captain and sent a captain's badge.

'Love is . . . .' began as a cartoon in the *Los Angeles Times* in 1973, and was serialized in the *Daily Express* in Britain. A whole series of 'Love is . . . .' badges was issued in various colours and sizes. Most were $1\frac{1}{2}$ in (38 mm) and were lithographed. In 1980 the *Daily Express* issued a set of $2\frac{1}{8}$ in (55 mm) lithographs commemorating Rupert Bear.

From 1950 to 1980 many national dailies disappeared through various takeovers and mergers, and the tabloids, such as the *Sun* and the *Mirror*, grew in popularity. At the time when many dailies were struggling, the *Express* decided to introduce a new daily similar in style to the tabloids. A big promotion helped the *Daily Star* off the ground in 1978, and included the $2\frac{1}{4}$ in (57 mm) badge, 'I'm a Daily Star gazer'. If you did not want to be a *Daily Star* gazer you could be a 'Guardian Whiz Kid', with a $2\frac{1}{8}$ in badge, or of course you could be both.

Newspaper clubs

Clubs for young readers were extremely popular before the war. Each had its own badge.

1 Bradford Telegraph and Argus Nig Nog Club. Unusual solid back on thin $\frac{3}{4}$ in (20 mm) button badge

2 Enamel of the *Leicester Mercury* Oozoos' Club, 1925 to 1939

3 1950s golly design of the *Bootle Times*

4 *News Chronicle* I Spy design pre-1961 and the *Daily Mail* takeover

5 Post-1961 design of the I Spy Club

6 *Daily Sketch* Pets' Cop of the late 1950s

7 to **17**, **19** to **23**, and **25** A variety of children's club designs from the 1950s to 1985. *21* and *22* use the same design. *17* is for the *Loughborough Echo*

18 What the papers say doesn't always please everyone. Around 1982 a Liberal who became a life peer hated the *Daily Express* so much that he had this design made up

24 Badge issued with the promotional launch of the *Daily Star* in 1978

26 *She* magazine promotion from the early 1980s

1

2

3

4

5

6

7

8

9

10

11

12

13

14

15

16

17

18

19

20

21

22

23

24

25

26

Comics

In the 1950s the popularity of the comic was in part due to a decline in children's clubs appearing in newspapers. Yet, by 1980, the popularity of the comic had declined in face of the onslaught of television. In the 1950s more than 12,000,000 comics were sold each week, compared with 5,500,000 in the mid-1970s and less than 3,000,000 in 1985. The bestseller by far in 1985 was the *Beano*, with an estimated circulation of 390,000, although this is way below its all-time peak of 600,000.

The launching of a new comic usually meant a free gift of some sort, and when it wasn't a cardboard clapper, or a plastic novelty, it was a badge. Comics such as the *Eagle*, *Lion*, and *Swift* for the boys, or *Girl* and *Robin* for the girls, conjure up images of pigtails, short trousers, and school caps in those (for the majority) pre-television days. Metal badges were usually given away with these comics, either as part of membership of a club or in the comic itself. One-inch (25 mm) button badges featuring *Eagle* characters such as Dan Dare and Jeff Arnold were given away in the 1950s.

Comics such as the *Eagle* and *Beano*, attracted cult followings in the 1970s and 1980s. In 1982 the *Eagle* was revamped and a plastic badge in the shape of an eagle was given away. Dennis the Menace, a hero for thousands of *Beano* readers, inspired the Dennis the Menace Fan Club in the late 1970s. Apart from young readers, many adults flocked to join and two badges were issued, a 2¼ in (57 mm) button badge featuring Dennis and a plastic badge of his dog Gnasher. Even television star Jimmy Crankie of the Crankies sports a Dennis the Menace Fan Club badge. The publishers of the *Beano*, D C Thomas of Dundee, also own the *Dandy*. The success of the Dennis the Menace Fan Club was followed up by the launch of a club for Desperate Dan, 'The Desperate Dan Pie Eaters Club'. A 2¼ in (57 mm) button badge was issued with a large hot pie in the centre, as well as a shaped plastic design featuring Dan's big head. A set of at least four Dandy characters was issued with the comic during the late 1970s—Desperate Dan, Beryl the Peril, Minnie the Minx, and Korky the Cat. In 1980 *Cheeky* comic issued a 'Friend of Cheeky' 1½ in (38 mm) button badge.

Over the years most comics have used badges of one kind or another for promotional purposes. Keen-eyed badge collectors survey the newsagents' stands for any giveaways. Popular comic characters, such as Dennis the Menace, also appear on many bootleg designs.

The decline of the comic market in the 1970s resulted in a battle for survival between the major comics. Apart from D C Thomas, the other big publisher in 1985 was IPC, and their deal with Weetabix saw the issue of a set of five designs in 1982 and four more in 1985. They were given away with comics such as *Whizzer and Chips*, *Tiger*, *Roy of the Rovers*, *Buster*, and *Tommy*.

IPC were also responsible, in the 1980s, for *2000 AD*, a comic which was described as the most important development since the *Eagle* was launched in the 1950s. Its theme reflected the computer age and American cultural influences. A 2⅛ in (55 mm) badge featuring 'Judge Dredd' was issued some time around 1980.

Comics

Comic characters appear on many badges.

1 Moulded plastic eagle for the comic's relaunch in 1982

2, **3** and **5** Formed metal comic badges

4 Jeff Arnold from 'The Riders of the Range' in the *Eagle* comic. It is believed this badge was given when a snake belt was purchased. This was a partner to a 1 in (25 mm) Dan Dare badge

6 Twinkle Club, a mid-1970s design by London Emblem Company

7 Dennis the Menace Fan Club, 1977 onwards

8 Paper and material Gnasher badge for the Dennis the Menace Fan Club

9 and **14** Desperate Dan's Club of the early 1980s. 9 is moulded plastic

10 *Roy of the Rovers* comic sponsored by Gola around 1983

11, **12** and **15** Three of a set of four *Dandy* characters given away with that comic in the late 1970s. The full set was: Korky the Cat, Beryl the Peril, Mini the Minx, and Desperate Dan

13 Readers of *Cheeky* could send for this design in 1980

16, **18** and **19** Club badge from magazines or journals

17 A badge given away with *Spiderman* comic in 1983

20 A badge free with the first issue of a new *Rupert* comic on October 1982

21 and **22** In the 1960s badges were given away with cereals. By 1982 cereal badges were given with comics! IPC comics such as *Tiger*, *Roy of the Rovers*, *Whizzer and Chips* had a deal with Weetabix which gave rise to a set of five badges (*22*) given away in 1982 and four more (*21*) in 1985

23 A badge given away with *Nutty* comic in 1983 which stars Bananaman

24 A badge from the comic *2000AD* featuring Judge Dredd, around 1979–1980

Libraries and books

In 1979 the Hertfordshire Library Service set about promoting children's libraries with badges. Their first badge was 'Books need people', $1\frac{3}{4}$ in (45 mm). This design and the others that followed proved popular and, eventually, what began as a local effort, spread throughout the length and breadth of Britain. From 1979 to 1985, 54 badges have been issued by the Hertfordshire Library Service, their aim being to produce three sets of three badges per year. The designs are so clever that, by 1985, 150,000 copies sold out quite quickly: 'Hop into a library' featuring a rabbit, and 'Coil up with a book' featuring a snake are two examples. Other libraries have also produced badges for promotion, but none so well as Hertfordshire whose badges can be found in most libraries nationwide. A team is employed to design them, and many of the ideas are sent in by children.

Book publishers have never been slow to use badges to promote their wares. 'The Famous Five Club' issued a $1\frac{1}{4}$ in (32 mm) design in the 1970s. Scholastic Books' Chip Book Club issued a $2\frac{1}{4}$ in (57 mm) 'I'm a chipmate' design around 1982. Other book clubs using badges include The Mickey Mouse Book Club and the Skylark Book Club.

Perhaps the biggest promotion of a book club was that for the Puffin books around 1982. Alongside their standard metal badge featuring the puffin was a $2\frac{1}{4}$ in (57 mm) button badge, 'The Puffin Promise a book for every child'. There are at least 10 others, all featuring puffins in one guise or another, such as the tennis puffin, 'Puffins are Ace'.

Other book promotions for children include 'Children's Book Week', sponsored by Lloyds Bank. Badges issued for this include the $1\frac{3}{4}$ in (45 mm) 'Bernard the Book Taster', a friendly monster. Lenny Henry helped to promote books and bookshops around 1982. 'What's at the end of a book? OK' featured Lenny Henry on a $2\frac{1}{4}$ in (57 mm) badge, and six $1\frac{1}{2}$ in (38 mm) designs showed a wise owl. Slogans such as 'Buy yourself a Book' and bookworm characters follow on from the library badges.

Other more specific book promotions since 1970 have featured characters from books on badges. From the mid-1970s onwards, character merchandizing became popular, and more badges depicting various characters appear. In the mid-1970s the *Mr Men* books by Roger Hargreaves were first published, and a new badge firm, Baynham Presswork, got hold of the copyrights. Mr Baynham had left the nearby Button Badge Company to start up on his own, and the Mr Men were just the start he needed. Huge quantities were sold, initially in a set of 26 $1\frac{1}{2}$ in (38 mm) designs, featuring all of the Mr Men. Later, a $2\frac{1}{8}$ in (55 mm) set was produced incorporating new characters.

After the mid-1970s Rainbow Design (London Emblem Company) and Baynham Presswork (now Baynham and Stanfield) produced sets of badges showing characters that, unlike the Mr Men, were not contemporary. Moreover, they included characters from books that had been made into films for the big or little screen.

Radio

At the same time as children's clubs developed in the newspapers they also began on the radio. In 1923 a little girl wrote to the Birmingham regional radio station suggesting the formation of a sort of radio pen pal circle. The Radio Circle which resulted helped link the children who listened in to those early *Children's Hour* broadcasts. The early badges of the Radio Circle show the station call sign only: London was 2LO and Birmingham was 5IT. By 1930 a standard badge showed the BBC logo with individual regional banners—London, North, Midlands, and so on. The 'sunbeams' design came from the Cardiff Radio Sunbeams. The annual subscription in 1930 was ninepence, and this included a free badge and a mention on the radio on your birthday. Ultimately this club was killed off because all 80,000 members expected their names to be read out on the air. H W Miller made most of the thousands of Radio Circle designs.

Comparatively few radio badges were made until the development of local radio. In 1967, after the pirate radio stations, came the reorganization of BBC radio. Radio One for the young (and old) rock and pop fans, has issued a variety of badges ever since its inception. Moreover, in the wake of the introduction of independent radio, the local BBC radio stations had to compete for listeners. Competition included maximum publicity and nearly every radio station produces a standard button badge. Their designs nearly always include the number of the station and prove an attractive thematic collection. Some local stations issue more badges than others, and often badges are awarded to winners of competitions. Capital Radio gave badges featuring signs of the zodiac to people who take part in programmes and thus become a 'Capital Radio Superstar'.

Some designs feature certain DJs and their programmes. It may be 'Melanie Parker gets me up in the morning' or 'It's bedtime Ian Fisher Late-on-show' (Radio Tees). The BBC stations usually include 'BBC' on their badges, and your local library will probably be able to supply you with a list of stations if you are not sure where they all are.

The Radio One Road Show usually has a badge, but like many in this field you will need to pay for it. Nearly all present radio designs are button badges, but some, including Radio Hallam and Pennine Radio, have issued plastics. Pennine Radio issued a moulded shaped plastic 'I'm a Radio Tyke' badge featuring a cartoon radioman.

Hospital radio, a very important service and found in most hospitals, often have badges which are usually sold to raise funds. Radio Lollipop, for children in hospital, issues badges for the young patients.

Radio

Until the recent promotional designs, radio has not been a major badge source.

1 and **4** Beautiful enamels made by H W Miller for the BBC Radio Circle in the 1920s and 1930s

2 and **3** Shaped moulded plastic promotional badges from the early 1980s

5 to **8** Designs for Radio 1. *6* is from the Radio 1 Club of the early 1970s. *8* is a plastic badge, one of at least three similar early Radio 1 promotional badges. Others include: 'I'm a Radio 1 one-upman' and 'Ring a 247 Ding Radio 1'

9 An interesting BBC local radio promotional lithograph of the 1970s

10 to **14**, **16**, **17** and **19** A variety of radio promotions from 1975 to 1985. *16* is one of a set issued by Capital Radio

15 and **18** Hospital radio badges

1

2

I'm a Radio Tyke

Pennine Radio 235mw 96 vhf

4

RADIO 1 ROAD SHOW

5

RADIO 1 CLUB

6

Tony Blackburn RADIO 1

7

go radio 1 better on 247

8

9

Swansea Sound 257 I'M TUNED IN

10

IT'S BEDTIME

RADIO TEES 257 METRES MEDIUM WAVE 96 VHF

IAN FISHER LATE-ON SHOW

11

BBC 224m RADIO ULSTER

12

HUM ALONG TO THE BBC MIDDAY CONCERTS

BBC-SSO

13

I'm an A.M. lover

JOIN ME - LBC's A.M. SHOW 261m.

14

RADIO LULLIPOP

The Hospital Radio for Children

15

CAPITAL RADIO SUPERSTAR

Pisces

16

BBC RADIO SHEFFIELD 290 AND VHF

17

HOSPITAL RADIO CHELMSFORD

18

STICK IT IN YOUR EAR

Theme music by Tom Scott & The L.A. Express

DJ: Brian Ford

RADIO CLYDE 261

19

147

Television's beginnings

Television is very important to the button badge story in Britain. Not only did it create an outlet for badges featuring the stars of the small screen, but it also created an advertising outlet, with many campaigns inevitably being influenced by TV trends. Similarly, the number of badges produced relates directly to the number of viewers. In the 1950s, when few people had sets, there were few badges, but by the 1980s when nearly everybody had a television set there were millions of badges.

One of the first television badges was for one of the first big television stars—Muffin the Mule. Muffin was purchased for 15 shillings by Ann Hogarth from a travelling salesman. Annette Mills spotted the puppet and became his presenter, while Ann Hogarth pulled the strings. In 1950 Annette Mills received the British Television Society's medal for the most outstanding contribution to television entertainment.

The Muffin Club was started in the weekly *TV Comic*, run by the *News of the World*, and five Muffin Club seals in the shape of a horseshoe had to be collected from the comic and sent with one shilling to join. Muffin was the first of what has proved to be a legion of children's heroes whose faces appear on badges.

After Muffin the Mule came Lenny the Lion, and Sooty and Sweep. Many of the late 1950s and early 1960s designs are $1\frac{1}{4}$ in (32 mm), and the Lenny the Lion Fan Club badge is instant nostalgia for those old enough to remember lovable Lenny. The *Sooty* show's original set of badges includes Butch and Kipper, two characters no longer in the show. Butch, a cheeky snapping dog, probably proved too much competition for the equally cheeky Sweep. The Sooty Friendship Circle dates from the early days of television.

In the early 1960s a children's programme started that found a winning formula. *Blue Peter* has been famous for many things; its presenters, its pets, its holidays and its appeals, and to this list must be added its badge. Indeed the badge was so famous, that in 1977 a punk version was produced featuring a man called Peter being throttled until he was blue. The standard *Blue Peter* badge is a white shield-shaped plastic badge with the ship in blue in the centre. Various others have been issued, including several thousand competition winner's badges. *Blue Peter* badges give free entry into certain museums and exhibitions. In order to get one, you have to do something really special, and thus they are not commonplace.

The ITV network's reply to *Blue Peter* was *Magpie*. *Magpie* did not prove to be quite as long-lived as *Blue Peter*, but their badges are just as interesting. They were awarded for letters or achievements relating to the theme song: 'One for sorrow, two for joy, three for a girl, and four for a boy, five for silver, six for gold, seven for a secret never to be told, eight for a wish, nine for a kiss, ten for a bird you must not miss'. As well as these 10 designs, all $2\frac{1}{8}$ in (55 mm) except for the last one which is $3\frac{1}{2}$ in (90 mm), there was a standard $2\frac{1}{8}$ in (55 mm) *Magpie* badge. When the programme came under threat of the axe there was a great response by viewers to keep it going and a $2\frac{1}{8}$ in (55 mm) badge 'Endangered Species—Magpie' was issued. However, it was to no avail and the programme disappeared from the national network.

Television: the early days

Children's programmes have issued badges since the earliest days of broadcasting.
1 Muffin the Mule Club badge of the early 1950s. The club cost one shilling to join along with five Muffin Club seals (horseshoe tokens) from *TV Comic*
2 Anglia began in 1959; this is a 1960s design
3 Lenny the Lion Fan Club badge
4 Standard shield-shaped plastic Blue Peter badge
5 Alternative Blue Peter badge
6 to **9** Part of a set of Sooty characters of the early 1960s. By 1985 Butch and Kipper were no longer in the show
10 Sooty Friendship Circle badge, 1960s
11 to **14**, and **17** Magpie badges. *12, 13* and *17* are from the set of 10, *17* is a $3\frac{1}{2}$ in (90 mm) frying pan
15 Petra, the Blue Peter programme's most famous pet, died on 14 September 1977 after appearing on the programme for 15 years. The book *Petra, a dog for everyone* was published in 1978 as was the badge
16 Crackerjack design of the 1970s

MUFFIN CLUB **1**

Anglia **2**

LENNY THE LION FAN CLUB **3**

4

THIS IS A BLUE PETER BADGE PETER **5**

SOOTY **6**

SWEEP **7**

KIPPER **8**

BUTCH **9**

SOOTY FRIENDSHIP CIRCLE **10**

11

3 FOR A GIRL MAGPIE **12**

4 FOR A BOY MAGPIE **13**

ENDANGERED SPECIES MAGPIE **14**

PETRA A dog for everyone **15**

Crackerjack JAN ED BERNIE PETER **16**

10 FOR A BIRD YOU MUST NOT MISS MAGPIE **17**

Television in the 1960s

In the 1960s the number of people watching television was growing rapidly. Children's cartoons became very popular, as they had done on the big screen. Hanna Barbera cartoons were imported from the United States including the characters Yogi Bear and Boo Boo, Mr Jinks and Pixie and Dixie, and Hucklebury Hound. Kellogg's and Hanna Barbera decided to give badges away with cereal packets. These were 1 in (25 mm) designs featuring the six characters, made up by B Sanders and Sons of Bromsgrove.

Other Yogi badges were issued in various ways later in the 1960s. They were usually $1\frac{1}{4}$ in (32 mm) and included 'Quick Draw McGraw', 'Fred Flintstone', and 'Wally Gator'. Batman, too, became a television star and in 1966 $1\frac{1}{4}$ in (32 mm) and $2\frac{1}{8}$ in (55 mm) badges were produced featuring him.

When the race into space during the 1960s reached fever pitch, space programmes for children were very popular. The space theme was reflected too on many advertising badges and some sets were made to accompany television series. The puppet programmes like *Stingray* and *Thunderbirds* also included in 1967 *Captain Scarlet of Spectrum*, and two sets of badges, one featuring the characters at $1\frac{1}{4}$ in (32 mm) and one featuring the spacecraft at $1\frac{1}{2}$ in (38 mm). In 1968 a set was produced for a similar puppet programme, *Joe 90 of WIN*, including Joe 90, Mac, Sam and a most special agent badge, issued on a $1\frac{1}{4}$ in (32 mm) button and also as a plastic shaped badge made in Hong Kong. Later a lithograph badge, 'Joe 90 7 years old' was produced.

In 1969 *Star Trek* became extremely popular. Kellogg's cereal again issued a set of badges and these included Captain Kirk, Dr McCoy, Sulu, Spock, and Star Trek captain. The BBC's own *Dr Who* was a runaway success in the 1960s, and plastic shaped Dalek badges were very popular. In 1971 the BBC issued a set of $1\frac{1}{4}$ in (32 mm) designs including Doctor Who (Jon Pertwee), Jo Grant, and Bessie (the car). In the later 1970s and 1980s *Doctor Who* became a cult programme and *Doctor Who* exhibitions were held, issuing a variety of badges including the logo and a 'Tardis Commander' badge.

Spies and private eyes were popular in the 1960s, too, and A & BC Bubble Gum issued a *Man From UNCLE* set of $\frac{7}{8}$ in (22 mm) button badges. Patrick McGoohan had become well known as *Danger Man* and shortly afterwards became *The Prisoner*. This series in the late 1960s, taken off the air before its time, later became a cult both in Britain and the United States. American Universities held Prisoner Conventions, and one Canadian University used the series as the basis for a sociology course. The Prisoner Appreciation Society was formed, and the famous badge which Patrick McGoohan wore as 'No 6' was copied and worn by thousands.

Other reminders of the 1960s' children's programmes are badges for the ATV Tingha and Tucker Club. The *TV Times* itself had its Tivvy Club, and a Rolf Harris Safari Club.

Television in the 1960s and 1970s

Popular TV characters became increasingly popular on badges.
1 to **5** The Yogi Bear set (minus Dixie) issued with cereal in the early 1960s, before the days of mass character merchandising in Britain
6 A Yogi Bear design of the late 1960s
7 A badge issued with 'UNCLE' bubblegum in the mid-1960s
8a and **8b** Batman became very popular in the mid-1960s, and this design was issued in two sizes in 1966. *8b* is one of a set of at least six Batman badges issued by A & BC chewing gum
9 to **11** Doctor Who designs. *9* is from the Doctor Who exhibition which appeared in various places in 1979–80. *11* is one of a set issued in 1971
12 and **13** Examples of two sets associated with Spectrum. *12* is from a 1967 set. *13* is from a lithographed set of at least five. Paint-filled metal examples of Spectrum also exist
14 to **16** Joe 90 designs. *14* is moulded plastic. *15* and *16* are from a 1968 set
17 and **18** A set of at least five *Star Trek* designs were given away with cereal in 1969
19, 20, 22 and **23** A variety of television clubs of the 1960s
21 Basil Brush design. A set was issued in 1977
24 Badge for a children's programme of the early 1980s
25 1977 badge from *The Prisoner*, a mid-1960s programme which developed a cult following

1

2

3

4

5

6

7

8

8

9

10

11

12

13

14

15

16

17

18

19

20

21

22

23

24

25

Television from the 1970s on

In the 1970s badge sets of television characters were issued in abundance. These included the Magic Roundabout and Camberwick Green (1972); The Wombles (over 3,000,000 sold) and Tom and Jerry (1975); The Muppets (1976); Fonz, Basil Brush, The Flumps, and Starsky and Hutch (1977); and Worzel Gummidge (1979). The character sets reached their peak around 1977 to 1979, when just about anything with a pin would sell. As well as the official sets which had copyrights, there were many bootlegs.

In the mid-1970s a new development in children's television was the Saturday morning show, piloted to a large extent by Noel Edmonds and the *Multi Coloured Swap Shop*. Most of the other programmes that developed along the same lines also issued badges. Programmes such as *Tiswas*, the *Mersey Pirate*, *Saturday Shake Up*, and *Saturday Superstore* all thrived for a time.

Other children's programmes, such as *Crackerjack*, *Runaround*, *Rainbow*, *Jigsaw*, *You and Me*, and *Roundabout* have issued badges. Such issues also include badges for the anniversaries of stations, or publicizing their programmes generally. Similarly, when a new station comes on the air, such as Channel 4, a badge is produced. '4 I've had my set set', was to encourage the public to make sure they could receive the new station. Reorganizations, such as the ITV shake-up in 1983, are also marked by badges: 'Westward TV into the 80s', 'Country comes West HTV', and 'Central goes East', are examples. Other ITV badges include seasonal ones such as 'Christmas on ITV', or 'Spring on ITV'. Many local news magazine programmes produce such button badges as 'Yorkshire Television Calendar Programme' and 'Tyne Tees Northern Life'. A particular programme anniversary may be marked by a badge such as BBC's '3000th Jackanory'. Other programmes using badges include ITV's '3 2 1' or BBC's 'Summertime Special' or ITV's 'Star Games'.

The soap operas boom of the late 1970s, in particular *Dallas*, provoked many designs, especially 'I love JR' or 'I hate JR', and 'JR Fan Club'. These included both button badges and moulded plastic designs. The development of video recorders, and the production of films for these, has seen a further batch of promotional badges for both the films and the video companies.

Television in the 1980s

Badges are standard issue today to accompany programmes, TV anniversaries and station promotions.

1 to 3 *Dallas* was the most popular programme in Britain in 1980. The programme's central character was loved or hated by millions. *2* is a shaped moulded plastic badge

4 Hilda Ogden and Kevin Turvey designs by Alien Pork Badges of Nottingham. Using hand machines of London Emblem Company and Universal Button Company, APB produced sets in 1984 for *Coronation Street*, *The Young Ones*, *Dr Who*, *Joe 90* and *Herman Munster*

5 to 8, **15** and **18** Badges commemorating television anniversaries, birthdays, or changes of status during the early 1980s

6 Sixty years of BBC's children's programmes, 1983

9, **10**, **12** and **16** Badges from Saturday morning children's television. Spit the dog became famous on *Tiswas*, a cult programme for children and adults alike from 1979 to 1982. *10* is from *The Saturday Banana*, an ITV programme hosted by Bill Oddie in 1978. To obtain this badge viewers had to send in one of their own. What happened to all the badges that were sent in?

11 Rolf Harris' Saturday Teatime badge, 1982

13 Rectangular designs of 1982. *Calendar* is a Yorkshire TV news programme

14 and **17** OWWRRAS, the Official World Wide Roland Rat Appreciation Society. Roland Rat came to the rescue of TVAM in 1983–4 after their disastrous start in breakfast television. *17* is an enamel, the logo for the initially more successful BBC *Breakfast Time* (by Toye, Kenning and Spencer)

15 Badge reminding people to set their television set to receive the new Channel 4 in 1982

Theatre

When button badges were just in their infancy at the turn of the century, the stars of the day were the stars of the theatre, especially the music hall. At this time the Whitehead and Hoag Company of Newark, New Jersey, USA, were issuing their first sets of badges, given away instead of cards with cigarettes. One of the biggest and commonest sets featured music hall artistes, and there were well over 240 in the set. Since many of these badges have turned up in Britain, and included British actresses such as Dorothy Dene and Ellen Terry and French actresses like Cleo de Merode, it is more than likely that Whitehead and Hoag were sounding out the European market. Some of the actresses appear on at least five different designs.

Apart from the very early examples, theatre badges before 1960 are rare. Since then badges relating to theatre have been issued for theatres and theatre companies, festivals, pantomimes, big productions, and theatrical celebrities, especially William Shakespeare. By 1970, with competition from television as well as cinemas, the theatres and their companies realized that they needed better publicity.

One annual pilgrimage that many make to the theatre is to a pantomime. The York Theatre Royal adopts a slogan for its pantomime badge, but there is no hint of the theatre or date on the design. In 1977–78 for their Cinderella production it was 'At midnight I turn into a pumpkin' and in 1978–79 'I'm all right, Jack' was for Jack and the Beanstalk. Other theatres choose to feature the star of their pantomime on the badge, like the Theatre Royal, Norwich with their 'Benny as Buttons—I luv's ye Cinders' design.

Theatres and theatre companies often produce anniversary badges, such as the 'Northern Ballet Theatre 10th Birthday 1969–1979' design. The National Theatre in London is just one of several modern theatres that issue badges.

Festivals, such as the Edinburgh Festival and York Festival of mystery plays, have badges. Edinburgh, in particular, produces designs for productions, especially for the fringe festival. For one Edinburgh production, *Thirteen Clocks*, a set of 13 1½ in (38 mm) badges was produced, each featuring a different clock. One theatre production that resulted in a lot of badges was *Joseph and the Amazing Technicolor Dreamcoat*. As well as spawning more badges for the various other productions of *Joseph*, it helped to establish a trend that for a big production, especially one that is suitable for the family, a badge is a must.

Badges featuring Shakespeare are not uncommon. A set in six colours with his face and the slogan 'Will Power' was very popular in the late 1970s, and many other Shakespeare designs are made for tourists to Stratford.

Travelling theatrical acts, such as magicians, often give out 'Magician's Assistant' badges, and these sometimes bear the name of the magician. Arts festivals and theatre or ballet workshops often issue badges, and one of the most obscure sets was issued through Welsh National Trust shops in 1977. This was a set of five Welsh writers— Waldo Williams, Oriel, D J Williams, T H Parry Williams and Dylan Thomas. Dylan Thomas was usually sold out.

The pop stars of their era, music hall artistes feature on early designs. Today badges are more likely to advertise productions.

1 to 8 Music hall artistes of the turn of the century. Over 240 badges were issued by the Whitehead and Hoag Company, with packets of cigarettes such as Sweet Caporal (*8*). Artistes featured were from the United States and Europe. Those shown are: Alice Evans (*1*), Lillian Relma (*2*), Della Fox (*3*), Pearl Revere (*4*), Clementine De Vere (*5*), Hope Booth (*6*), Helen Bartram (*7*)

9 to 26 Theatre designs from 1970 to 1985. *10* is part of a set of five different colours (White and Lambert). *15* is part of a set of 13 clocks, for a production at the Edinburgh Festival. *16* is part of a set of seven deadly sins. *17* is D J Williams, one of a set of five Welsh poets

18 A badge bearing the magician's name on an insert, Wal Mayne of Borehamwood

22 A Badge Shop design for Godspell

23 From York Theatre Royal pantomime, 1978–9

Cinema

Before the war a silver brooch badge of Mickey Mouse was produced and today this is much sought after. Walt Disney badges since then have been plentiful, and the Disney copyright is usually in evidence. Many Disney characters featured on sets by Rainbow Design are post-1975. Individual Disney films issued badges on their first showing in Britain during the 1950s and 1960s, a time when cinema badges first became common in Britain. Of these 1950s' Disney issues 'Davy Crockett' is featured on a 1 in (25 mm) design, wearing that famous coonskin hat. The popularity of cowboy films is confirmed on a badge featuring 'Hopalong Cassidy and Topper' for a film called *Boston*.

Many of these badges were given or sold during the Saturday morning cinema clubs for children. The ABC Cinema was one of the biggest and their club the ABC Minors, produced many classic button badges for this period.

The ABC Minors issued a whole series of 1 in (25 mm) designs such as Windsor Castle, a guardsman, and Coco the Clown at Bertram Mills Circus. Monitors were appointed and given badges of merit. Badges were also issued for certain films, such as *Lassie*. Standard designs incorporating the triangular logo were issued in at least five colours, and had a luminous centre to shine inside the dark cinema. Later issues were a standard non-luminous design and an identical badge with a luminous ring round the outside. Star Cinema Juniors Club also issued a 1¼ in (32 mm) design featuring a luminous star. In the mid-1960s the luminous design was dropped by ABC and replaced by a set of nine badges, each with a different letter on it, the set spelling out ABC MINORS. These were mostly manufactured by J R Gaunt of Birmingham. In the early 1970s 'EMI Saturday Show' and 'ABC Cinema Minors Matinee' designs of 1½ in (38 mm) crimped were made by White and Lambert in green, blue, yellow and pink. A 2¼ in (57 mm) design was issued in 1972 featuring that famous 'Smily' face.

The Boys' and Girls' Cinema Club was the original title of the Odeon Cinema Club. Their standard design features the man banging the gong; a 1¼ in (32 mm) silver and red design was being issued in 1954. Later designs were 1 in (25 mm) red and white. In the late 1960s the club became the Odeon Saturday Club and a 1½ in (38 mm) badge, 'There's lots of fun at the Odeon Saturday Club' was issued.

Since the days of the Saturday cinema clubs, badges have been issued for certain films and film stars. In 1976 Tantra Designs issued a set of over 30 film stars in sepia, following the fashion for nostalgia. From Charlie Chaplin to John Wayne, badges of film stars are common in the United States but almost unknown in Britain. Blockbusting films of the late 1970s and early 1980s that were accompanied by sets of badges include *Grease*, *Superman*, *ET* and the *Life of Brian*. The Lone Ranger even turns up on badges but these were produced for a 1981 film and not the original TV series.

Most of the sets for the box office giants of 1976 to 1985 are button badges, but notably a plastic shaped Superman badge proved very popular with fans of the film.

Clubs, stars and films feature on cinema badges.

1 to **11**, and **13** ABC Minors Cinema Club badges from the early 1950s to mid-1970s. *1* is part of a set with a luminous white area. *2* has a luminous ring instead of a colour. *3* is one of a late 1960s set by Gaunt, which spelt out ABC MINORS. *4*, and *7* to *11* are 1950s badges from films or for monitors. *4* sports what was probably the original logo, which also appears on a 1¼ in (32 mm) design. *5* is another late 1960s non-luminous design by Gaunt. *6* is one of a set of four different coloured 1970s badges by White and Lambert

12 Luminous star of the Star Junior Club, late 1950s

14 to **16** Badges for Odeon Boys' and Girls' Club, which by the late 1960s had become the Saturday Club

17 to **19**, **21** to **23** Badges from various films of the 1950s and 1960s, mainly Walt Disney

20 Much sought-after prewar Mickey Mouse badge

24 to **27** Buster Keaton, Harpo Marx, Marlon Brando, and Marilyn Monroe respectively, from a mid-1970s set of 32 film stars by Tantra Designs

28 to **32** Badges from recent films. *28* is from a 1978 set of at least eight published by Factors Etc and made up by Baynham and Stanfield. *30* is from a set of seven badges for the *Life of Brian* published by Big Time Promotions in 1980. *32* is from a 1982 set of at least eight published by Star Power

Rock and pop: the early days

In 1953 a number called *Crazy Man Crazy* by a group called Bill Haley and the Comets, became the first rock and roll record to enter the American charts. Their follow-up in 1954, a song called *Rock Around the Clock* was unsuccessful, but when it was reissued in 1955, as the title music to the film *The Blackboard Jungle,* it became a world-wide smash hit. Rock had arrived.

The first real superstar, however, was Elvis Presley. It was Elvis whom millions of badges were made. Colonel Parker, Presley's shrewd manager, hit on the idea of selling millions of 'I love you Elvis' badges to the girls and then proceeded to double his money by selling 'I hate you Elvis' to their boyfriends. If the quantity of Elvis designs in the 1950s was big, it was nothing compared to those produced in 1977 when he died.

Since those early days of rock, badges have been produced in massive quantities. These include badges for official fan clubs, official tours, record promotions, new artists, and those of 'flavour of the month' pop stars which are sold through retail outlets. Early rock and roll badges, featuring Buddy Holly, Eddie Cochran and Cliff Richard and the Shadows, are rare, however.

While millions of badges are produced at the height of a star's career, they very quickly disappear when he or she does. However, since the badge explosion of 1977, badges of the superstars of rock, such as Elvis, Bowie, The Beatles, Dylan, Hendrix, Clapton, and the Rolling Stones, have been reproduced in many forms.

Beatlemania in the 1960s is very important to the development of badge wearing. Children who grew up in the 1950s wearing Dan Dare badges, ABC Minors Cinema Club badges and the advertising badges of that period were now ready for teenage badges. These 'fab gear' badges of the 1960s grew into the 'If you had it last night smile' innuendoes of the 1970s and 1980s.

Several million Beatles badges were made in the heyday of Beatlemania, but they are now rare. A set of plastic shaped guitars with their faces in the centre was issued around 1964. Large $3\frac{1}{2}$ in (90 mm) frying pans were also issued featuring The Beatles' faces and the Beatle logo, and 'With love from me to you' around the top of the badge. Shaped plastic and metal beetles were also made. A black and white $1\frac{1}{4}$ in (32 mm) set was issued in 1965, but the most common Beatles' badges are post-1977 reproductions of LP covers.

The groups that followed on from the Beatles all had badges, and many were shown on a set that was issued in large quantities: 'I like the . . . . . .', $1\frac{1}{4}$ in (32 mm) button badges with a white background and featuring most of the popular groups of 1964 and 1965. Another 'I like . . . . .' set was issued by A and BC Bubble Gum in 1966. As well as the Beatles, these included The Monkees, a product of television. The Rolling Stones had some 3 in (75 mm) frying pans which used black and white photographs, and these badges include one of Brian Jones, their guitarist who died in 1969.

The Kinks were to be one of the longer lasting groups. Badges with the face of Ray Davies and other members of the group appeared, and 'God save the Kinks', a $2\frac{1}{8}$ in (55 mm) design, was issued with their LP *Arthur* in America and later sold at concerts in Britain.

The early days of rock

An essential accessory for the fan of the 1960s was the badge.
1 and **2** Original moulded plastic foil-tipped guitar-shaped badges of The Beatles
3 and **4** Not original designs but produced, like many others of rock stars, since 1977. *3* is one of millions sold when Elvis died. *4* is Buddy Holly, one of a set issued by Tantra Designs
5 to **10**, **12**, **17** and **18** Original 1960s designs. *9* is one of a set of $3\frac{1}{2}$ in (90 mm) frying pans, lithographs with solid backs. *6* to *8* are also part of a set. *18* is one of the many designs of the Monkees and Beatles issued with A & BC Bubble Gum. *10* and *12* are 3 in (77 mm) Rolling Stones frying pans
11 A 1977 solid back lithograph of the Beatles *Sergeant Peppers* album. Most of the Beatles LP covers received this treatment in 1977–8
13 to **16**, **19** and **20** 1984 $\frac{3}{4}$ in (19 mm) designs made by Alien Pork Badges, of Nottingham using Universal Button Company machine and parts. *13* to *16* are from *Help* and were also sold at Beatle museums
21 The *Sergeant Peppers* album kit included two card badges, one of which was reproduced on this lithograph in the early 1970s
22 Kinks design issued in the United States with their LP *Arthur* and sold at concerts in Britain

Rock and pop in the 1970s

The Who represented the 'mods', a subculture whose members were distinguished by battles with their enemies, the rockers, and who had flags on their scooters, sew-on badges on their parkas and button badges on their lapels. Mod badges, however, are commoner from 1979 onwards when The Jam helped to revive the trend. The mod badges of the 1960s were more often of the 'philosophical' nature.

A set of $1\frac{1}{4}$ in (32 mm) designs during the 1960s were take-offs of top songs of the day, thus 'I was Kaiser Bill's Batman' by Whistling Jack Smith became 'Who was Lord Kitchener's valet?', and 'Everyone's gone to the Moon' by Jonathan King, became 'Keep the Pope off the Moon'.

The late 1960s saw the flower power movement at its prime, and in the United States the three-day Woodstock Festival on 21 August 1969 was attended by some 450,000 fans. Millions of 'love and peace' badges were made to add to the badge boom of the 1960 and 1970s. The 'underground' movement of the late 1960s saw badges being issued for groups such as Led Zeppelin, Cream, Jethro Tull and later Derek and the Dominoes, including a 'Derek is Eric' badge (Eric Clapton).

During the period 1971 to 1977 the more serious 'underground' groups as they became known, concentrated on LPs and loud tours, and pop became a dirty word. Teenybop and 'bubblegum' music became the chart material, and groups such as The Osmonds and David Cassidy were attracting younger and younger fans. 'I love Donny' and 'I love Jimmy' badges were produced in a range of loud, fluorescent colours. Moody Motifs Boogie Buttons supplied a set of 2 in (50 mm) coloured drawings of stars including Jimmy Osmond, Donny Osmond, David Cassidy, The Sweet, Rod Stewart, Gary Glitter, Gilbert O'Sullivan, Slade, Alice Cooper, and Cat Stevens.

Coffer of London also put out several $2\frac{1}{4}$ in (57 mm) photographic designs, including a very young-looking David Bowie. Coffer also issued $3\frac{1}{2}$ in (90 mm) frying pans featuring a very young Michael Jackson. Splash Badges included Marc Bolan in their designs. From an 'underground' star with Tyrannosaurus Rex, Bolan had become a teenybop idol with T Rex.

By 1975 the teenybop scene reached its peak with the tartan scarves and pretty faces of the Bay City Rollers. Rollermania became the biggest thing to hit British pop music since The Beatles. Bill Merton and Phil Coulter, who had composed *Puppet On A String* for Sandie Shaw, wrote most of the Bay City Roller's hits. The ephemeral nature of such groups means that their badges are fairly rare because, although millions were made, millions were also thrown away.

Pop in the 1970s

Badges took on a more devotional note in the teenybop days of the 1970s

1 One of several alternative title badges, this one comes from the single *I was Kaiser Bill's Batman* by Whistling Jack Smith
2 Woodstock happened in August 1969, and the film was seen by millions
3 to **5** Mods and Rockers, motorbikes and scooters, and Bank Holiday seaside battles—echoes of the mid-1960s
6 Metal Led Zeppelin badge
7 to **9** The Osmonds 1972 badges
10 to **12** Badges from sets by Coffer of London around 1970 showing a young David Bowie (*10*) and an even younger Michael Jackson (*11*), and Slade (*12*)
13 and **14** Two of a set by Moody Motifs Boogie Buttons showing artistic impressions of Gary Glitter (*13*) and Sweet (*14*) around 1973
15 Marc Bolan, 1972
16 The Bay City Rollers, by Coffer, London

The rise of punk

One group that emerged in the 1970s to give pop a bit more respectability was the Swedish group Abba. Having won the Eurovision Song Contest in 1974, their slick pop style and strong melodies ensured chart-topping success. Millions of badges were produced, many $2\frac{1}{8}$ in (55 mm) with solid backs.

'Underground' groups who performed live often issued tour badges and group badges. These include Yes, Genesis, Led Zeppelin, Pink Floyd, Free, Deep Purple, Groundhogs, and Jethro Tull. For his 1976 UK tour Elton John issued a badge 'Louder than Concorde but not quite as pretty'.

Partly as a backlash to 'glam' rock and the commercialism of pop, a new culture was emerging in 1976 which became manifest in 1977 as punk rock. Punk had a tremendous effect on the button badge trade. Badges were very much in, and in London in 1977 people would stand outside tube stations selling badges from huge boards. Of the millions sold, many had little or nothing to do with punk rock. It was almost as if anything with a pin on would sell.

Apart from badges featuring punk stars, especially the Sex Pistols, badges were sold featuring every other type of rock performer from the past, from Buddy Holly to Bob Marley. Everyone, it seemed, wanted a badge depicting their favourite. Badges in bad taste were also part of punk culture. The Clash were one of the more popular punk bands and, under contract to CBS, they were forced to issue a single called *Remote Control* which they did unwillingly. They then wrote *Complete Control* which CBS backed and a badge 'I want complete control' was issued.

Ian Dury set something of a trend when, in conjunction with his record *Sex and Drugs and Rock and Roll*, he issued five badges to be worn together, all 1 in (25 mm) that said 'Ian Dury &', 'Sex &', 'Drugs &', 'Rock &', and 'Roll &'. Other groups have also used this idea.

Better Badges of London was one of the companies that sprang up to meet the punk demand for various items, especially badges. Founded by a 'hippy', Jolyon Macfie, Better Badges began in the summer of 1976, and their first success bore the motto 'Pass it this way' under a motif of crossed joint and hash pipe. 'Hendrix lives' was another good early seller, but within a few weeks it was 'Anarchy in the UK'. Better Badges became successful because they filled a huge gap in the market. Until this time badges had either been made via major record companies and given away as a promotional aid, or made by a merchandizing company and sold at that particular band's concerts.

Initially Better Badges gave bands a certain number of badges free; later they offered a discount rate. Apart from millions of badges made for little-known bands, Better Badges also produced designs for groups who later became supergroups. The Police are an example. When the Police were unknown, Better Badges made their first badge and gave them 1,000 free; later, of course, millions of Police badges were sold.

Other designs were being made for punk bands all over Britain as the craze spread. Often these were produced in small quantities on hand-operated machines, sold to meet this demand. The large music shops would have boards with literally thousands of badges to choose from. A good collection is often a reminder of bands who have long since disappeared.

The rise of punk

The badge boom of the late 1970s coincided with punk
1 Mid-1970s Roxy Music design
2 Promotion for a Yes LP
3 Badge from Elton John's 1976 tour
4 One of many designs featuring Abba
5 Millions of Elvis badges were sold in 1977 after his death
6 Millions of Sex Pistols badges were sold, too, and this one is part of a set published by Taylorscope and made up by Baynham and Stanfield
7 to 18, 20 and 21 A selection of designs from the late 1970s. *13* is Elvis Costello. *15* is a badge issued by The Clash. *16* is The Jam. *17* is an early Adam and the Ants badge. *21* is the Ian Dury set
19 One of millions of $2\frac{1}{2}$ in (65 mm) frying pans sold in 1977 featuring stars of the past as well as of the present, a lithograph with solid back

1   2   3   4

5   6   7

8   9   10   11   12   13

14   15   16   17   18

19   20   21

Rock and pop in the 1980s

In the wake of punk, badges generally became smaller. Vast quantities of 1 in (25 mm) designs were produced. Mirror badges were popular for about 18 months, as were glitter or reflective designs. One of the commonest subjects for these was Debbie Harry of Blondie. Many Marilyn Monroe badges were also in evidence.

Rock memorabilia grew once again as several famous stars died, such as Marc Bolan, Sid Vicious, Bill Haley and Bob Marley. The murder of John Lennon in December 1980, in the same way as the death of Elvis in 1977, created much media attention as well as saddening a whole generation. Owners of hand-operated machines were quick to react, and on the very afternoon of Lennon's death the Badge Shop in London were making up memorial badges.

The Specials, Madness, and the Jam ushered in a mod revival. One-inch (25 mm) button badges were made in the millions. Many of these designs incorporated the Union Jack. A new generation of mods on scooters could be seen on Bank Holiday weekends heading for seaside resorts, laden with 1 in (25 mm) button badges.

Groups with mass popular appeal, such as the Police, Status Quo, Queen, and many heavy metal groups, had badges on sale at retail outlets through this period. Other groups, such as Showaddywaddy, came and went. Other forms of rock, such as reggae and heavy metal, had their champions and for these fans thousands of badges were made. In 1982 'Bubble Pops', consisting of a package like a matchbox which included two plastic badges and some bubble gum, were available. The badges featured stars from punk to heavy metal, from the Clash to Bad Manners, Spandau Ballet, Adam Ant, the Stray Cats, and Saxon. Other moulded plastic designs of this time included some that simply stated the group's name.

In the 1980s Duran Duran and Wham proved that good-looking lads could still make it big, and thousands of badges featuring them were sold. Similarly, Michael Jackson's phenomenal record sales were equalled by badge sales.

Other music badges include those for the music press and television. Magazines, such as *Smash Hits*, have often given away badges with their issues. Festivals and concerts, such as Reading Rock Festival and Cambridge Folk Festival, also issue badges. Rock itself became increasingly involved in politics in the 1970s with 'Rock against Racism', and in the 1980s with charity work. Bob Geldof of the Boomtown Rats, initiated the Band Aid appeal for Ethiopia with a record released for Christmas, 1984; in 1985, the Live Aid concerts raised over £40,000,000.

Since the beginning of the punk era, badges featuring every rock star since Bill Haley have been made. The increase in the number of badge-making machines has further spread the number of designs. Reproductions of 1950s and 1960s groups on badges, have also sold heavily as rock memorabilia developed. Alien Pork Badges of Nottingham made up designs in 1984, including $\frac{3}{4}$ in (19 mm) designs with a stick pin featuring The Beatles.

Rock into the 1980s

The trend today is for smaller badges.

1, 2 and **6** 2½ in (65 mm) solid-backed safety-pinned frying pans prevalent in 1977–8, featuring all sorts of popular artists including Showaddywaddy, Marilyn Monroe and Status Quo. The Marilyn badge is a lithograph with solid back

3 In 1978–9 Debbie Harry of Blondie was being compared with Marilyn Monroe. Among the millions of badges made many were reverse printed mirrors in a plastic base

4 The Northern Soul scene produced many sew-on patches and a few button badges

5 Badge for BBC's long running rock programme *The Old Grey Whistle Test*

7 Sid Vicious of the Sex Pistols died in 1979

8 Another premature death was that of Bob Marley in 1981. This badge is in Rastafarian colours

9 Bill Haley also died in the early 1980s

10 to **31** From 1981 to 1985 the 2½ in (64 mm) frying pans all but disappeared and smaller badges became popular. Millions of 1 in (25 mm) designs were sold from boards at tube stations, record shops and fashionable places. *12* is a second-surface printed insert. *14* is an enamel badge. *20* was published by Better Badges who have produced millions of rock badges since 1977. *25* and *26* are moulded plastics sold with bubblegum as 'Bubble pops' in 1982. *28* is Nik Kershaw. *29* is Michael Jackson. *30* is a Duran Duran design which uses the heart symbol. *31* is Paul Young

Philosophical and decorative designs

Since the swinging sixties, badges have been worn just for amusement or fashion. **A** product initially of the Beatle era, when anything was fair game, the trend has grown ever since. Psychedelic badges in fluorescent colours were one example. The punk culture gave rise to bad taste badges, some of which have led to prosecution.

Many of these designs relate to sex, drugs and alcohol. In the 1960s most badges were fairly harmless: 'Boy wanted', 'Girl wanted', 'Satisfaction guaranteed', and 'Sock it to me' were all common. More intellectual designs were 'Shakespeare ate Bacon', and 'Forget Oxfam feed Twiggy'. A yellow design with the word 'Love' was also common in the early 1970s, featuring that familiar 'Smily' face. 'You don't have to be mad to work here but it helps' is another example. 'I like the Maharajah', a design from 1968, reflects a time when the Beatles were in India and pot smoking was an increasing trend with the young.

'Please f f fondle me, member of the Anglo Saxon stutterers club' is another late-1960s example of sexual innuendo. Many of these badges were sold or given away at amusement parks or fairgrounds. Badges of boys' and girls' names and signs of the zodiac were popular between 1966 and 1972. One zodiac set was by Moody Motifs Boogie Buttons, and were lithographed $2\frac{1}{8}$ in (55 mm) gold and black designs. Many other astrological sets exist, including one by Tantra, 1975.

The demand for 'philosophy' badges proved so high in the 1970s that a Japanese firm produced some designs and exported them to Britain. The problem was these very rough $2\frac{1}{8}$ in (55 mm) lithographs had a very inadequate stick pin fastening and several words were misspelled, as in 'Good By cruel world'. Other designs in this interesting set include 'Have car will park, Have wife must travel', 'Work is the curse of the drinking classes' and 'Cheer up the first 100 years are the hardest'.

Another set of lithographs was issued at fairgrounds and similar places in the early 1970s. This set included 'International Bull Shippers Assoc.', 'Just passin thru', 'Keep on truckin', 'Rock and Roll', 'I'm stoned', 'This space for rent', '69', 'Nice one', 'The Red Baron', 'I'm a genius', 'Mushroom' and the Rolling Stone logo of a tongue sticking out.

BOY WANTED

1

Please F-F-FONDLE me · MEMBER OF THE ANGLO SAXON STUTTERERS CLUB ·

2

I LIKE THE MAHARAJAH

3

AN APPLE FOR MY TEACHER

4

Frank

5

Rosemary

6

SOCK IT TO ME

7

KATHY

8

Keep on Truckin'...

9

SATISFACTION GUARANTEED

10

LOVE

11

12

HAPPY DAYS

13

TRY IT YOU'LL LIKE IT

14

INTERNATIONAL BULL SHIPPERS ASSOC.

15

SAGITTARIUS

16

GOOD·BY·CRUEL WORLD!" JAPAN

17

WORK IS THE CURSE OF THE DRINKING CLASSES JAPAN

18

HOME GROWN

19

Trendy messages

Art and lettering styles also invoke the past. The lettering on a $2\frac{1}{2}$ in (64 mm) design 'Go fly yourself a plane', and a $2\frac{1}{8}$ in (55 mm) 'Nice one', very definitely brings back memories of flared trousers. Other popular designs of that time include the American and British flags. The victory hand symbol was popular around 1970, and Uncle Sam pops up pointing his finger like Kitchener and stating 'Have you taken your pill today?' (Splash badges). In 1979 a $2\frac{1}{8}$ in (55 mm) design had a small pill inserted between the acetate and the print and the message 'The Pill—in emergency break wrapper'. Similarly, two $2\frac{1}{2}$ in (64 mm) 1977–78 designs featured one penny pieces. On one were the words 'Penny for your thoughts' and on the second 'In emergency break glass'.

Tantra Designs, begun by Pete Douglas in the early 1970s, initially produced 36 badges featuring 'Tantra', an Indian religion. These were mostly worn as decorative or fashionably 'far out' accessories. Tantra produced other sets, including: Celtic paintings, mushrooms, and many other magical and mystical designs. They also produced sets featuring rock stars, ecological, film stars, and many others. These badges sold in massive quantities in boutiques, bookshops, and the other new retail outlets that developed in the 1970s.

In 1977, with punk, large $2\frac{1}{2}$ in (64 mm) designs, often lithographs with a solid back and safety pin, were sold mostly from large boards outside tube stations. Many of these reached the height of bad taste, but it was two years later that they became really offensive. 'This is a Blue Peter badge' and 'Horatio Nelson was 'armless', are tame 1977 examples. Adolf Hitler was featured in a series of $2\frac{1}{2}$ in (64 mm) designs, and 'Bored teenager' the cliché of 1977, became that year's biggest selling badge.

Skateboarding was another craze in 1977. Sets of skateboarding badges were issued by Rainbow Designs (London Emblem Company), and Taylorscope (Baynham and Stanfield).

In 1977 it was any excuse for a badge. One design summed this up. It was sold in a box on which it was written 'For someone who has everything'. When you opened the box there was a badge which simply said 'I've got everything'. Frying pans of over 5 in (128 mm) were prizes at one fairground, showing a cuddly dog and stating 'Love me'. Another frying pan of 4 in (102 mm) states 'A penny saved won't buy owt anyhow'. One girls' magazine issued a heart-shaped plastic badge which had a removable plastic disc enabling the wearer to change the message on the badge.

Trendy messages and decorative designs: 1970s

Cute sayings and jokes sell well.
1 to **3** Late 1960s designs. *2* and *3* are both lithographs
4 to **9** Tantra Designs issued several sets in the mid-1970s. *4* is from a set of Aztec paintings. *5* is a badge in the Celtic set. *7* is from the Tantra set of 36 badges. *8* is from a set of 25 Red Indians. *9* is from a set of 14 onomatopoeia
10 and **11** Splash badges issued 'Have you taken your pill today?' (*10*) in the mid-1970s, and just in case you hadn't *11* was issued in 1980, in which a 'pill' was sealed under the acetate
12 Plastic heart with interchangeable messages issued with a teen-magazine in the late 1970s
13 1977 design sealing a penny behind the acetate
14 and **15** From two Rainbow Designs sets of the mid-1970s
16 A badge issued by a Suffolk toy company in 1980 and sold in gift shops complete with box
17 and **20** Two frying pans of the punk era were being sold from boards in London streets at 40p each or three for £1.00. *17* was part of a 'Hitler' set, which quickly vanished as anti-Nazi feeling grew
18 1977's bestselling badge
19 The 'Smily' face was still going strong on this 1978 White and Lambert crimp

Questionable taste

Around 1979 in Bristol, The Bristol Button Badge Company, under the name West Country Marketing and Advertising Ltd, were packaging 87 'philosophical' designs for retail outlets all over Britain. These included many that became very big sellers. 'Muffin the Mule is not a criminal offence', 'I am not a pheasant plucker', 'You need leather balls to play rugby', 'Could I see Uranus tonight?', 'Drink varnish — it'll kill you but you'll get a lovely finish', 'If God had wanted us to fly he'd have given us tickets', and 'Save gas fart in a money box', are some of the milder examples of a set that sold heavily into the 1980s. Jolyon Macfie, the boss of Better Badges, explained, 'The badge renaissance is largely the product of the music business. Punk attitudes have been succeeded by a sense of rebel without a cause'.

By 1979 there had already been one prosecution for wearing an obscene badge under the Vagrancy Act. The culprit was a Liverpool girl who, while standing at a bus stop, sported a badge promoting a record by the rock band, Wayne County: 'If you don't want to f . . . me baby, then f . . . off'.

In November 1980 a magistrate, Mrs Anne Evans, while travelling by tube, was confronted by a youth wearing an obscene badge. When she asked him to remove it, he replied, 'Why should I?'. Mrs Evans was further angered when no one else on the train backed her up. Mrs Mary Whitehouse of the National Viewers and Listeners Association blamed the government for the rapidly declining moral standards of the nation: 'We see the realms of acceptability being pushed back in many fields—the making and wearing of obscene badges is just one.' Under the 1824 and 1838 Vagrancy Acts 'It is an offence for a person wilfully to expose to view in any public place any obscene print, picture or indecent exhibition', and this includes shops as well.

In 1982 the top 70 bestselling badges were supplied by Scandecor to major retail outlets (including Woolworths), and included pop and philosophical badges. The designs included 'My brain hurts', and 'Sex appeal, please give generously'.

Other designs showed far better taste. Rainbow Designs produced a set of 1 in (25 mm) designs of illustrations by Kim Lane, as well as sets of roly poly ladies and coy little girls, in conjunction with the Bamforth Company.

In 1979 a $2\frac{1}{4}$ in (57 mm) badge was produced with a sticker saying 'Make the most of the 70s, peal off at midnight'. When the sticker was pealed off, 'I'm into the 80s' was revealed. Into the 1980s the badge was still in demand, such as the Union Jack design featuring a Japanese gentleman saying 'Buy Blitish'. In 1982 Rubik's cube was the rage. A $1\frac{3}{4}$ in (45 mm) badge stating 'I can do the cube' was issued with some of the cubes—surely an optimistic badge!

Novelty badges from the United States ranged from Star Wars designs, in which flashing lights were worked by a microcircuit and batteries, to badges which played a tune such as 'Happy Birthday' or Christmas songs. Heat-sensitive badges, which changed colour at the touch of warm fingers, liquid crystal badges which worked in a similar way, and a host of reflective or glitter badges were being made in the 1980s to add interest and glamour to the market.

Messages for the 1980s

1 and **2** December 1979 issues. Peel off the sticker on *1* to reveal *2*
3 Plastic clip-on style badge, 1979
4 One of a set of at least 12 Kim Lane drawings issued through Rainbow Designs, 1979
5,**7**, **9** to **20** A selection of a 1979 set of 87 designs sold through major retail outlets (Bristol Buttons, West Country Marketing and Advertising)
6, **8**, **21** and **25** Similar 'philosophical' designs issued during the same period
22 A reminder of the Rubik's cube craze, 1981–2
23 Liquid crystal novelty badge
24 Reflective novelty badge
26 A reminder of the skateboard craze 1977–9, one of Rainbow Design's set of at least six badges

Birthdays

Birthday badges probably originated from school badges. Designs stating simply 'Birthday' in a bar across the badge first appeared in schools well before the 1960s.

In the 1960s manufacturers came to realize that putting a badge on a birthday card was a good idea—they would sell more cards and also more badges. This became commonplace in the 1970s. Nearly all the earlier badges are 1 in (25 mm) but in the mid-1970s 1¼ in (32 mm) and 2⅛ in (55 mm) badges became common. By the 1980s, five standard designs were being used, all stating the obvious. By far the most popular is the one which says, for example, 'I am 7'.

Originally, the vast majority of these badges were white print on a red background, but today designs are more colourful. Print style and size varies greatly. Many are lithographs although the greater majority are acetates. Several manufacturers make birthday badges and they have even been imported from Hong Kong. Other unusual lithograph badges are simply flat discs with a fold-over fastening, the ultimate in cheap design. Other glitter or reflective badges are designed to catch the eye. One manufacturer, name unknown, made a grammatical blunder on designs which read 'I am 6 year old', and so on. Perhaps these were made abroad.

In 1984 Elphick Designs had the novel idea of using the same design on the badge as on the card. These were among the first birthday badges to incorporate a design.

The commonest ages for birthday badges are between four and nine. It is considered dangerous for babies of one- or two-year-olds to wear button badges; similarly, the ages 11 and 12 are rare, although Baynham and Stanfield produced a set for sale separately from cards which went up to twelve. London Emblem Company have produced 'I am 21', and 'I am 18' badges as well as '50 today', which the recipient will probably hesitate to wear before being fortified by a few birthday drinks!

Birthday badges

1 and **2** School birthday badges
3 Lithograph of the late 1970s
4 Stick-pin lithograph—stick pins can be dangerous for young children
5 An early greetings card badge of the late 1960s
6 A lithograph with an inadequate 'fold over' fixing
7 to **12**, **14** to **16**, and **18** General card issues from 1969 to 1983. Types such as 9 were common from 1969 to 1977. *12* is a glitter design, 1980. *16* is a wrongly spelt design. *18* is unusual; big badges with big pins are deemed unsuitable for babies
13 and **17** Badges sold separately from the card. *13* is a 1985 Rainbow Design issue. *17* is a Baynham and Stanfield 1982 issue
19 By 1983 brighter colours were in demand
20 Elphick Designs issued badges which formed part of the card design in 1984. These also have a solid back safety-pin fixing, more suitable for babies
21 Paddington Bear set by Rainbow Designs 1982

Character merchandizing

By the 1970s the age of character merchandizing had arrived. Rainbow Designs were one of the first companies to see the possibilities and from their early beginnings in 1971, they developed rapidly to become leaders in the field, issuing dozens of series of badges. Initially they had their designs made up by other manufacturers such as B Sanders and Sons of Bromsgrove, but by 1975 they set up their own manufacturing unit, the London Emblem Company. The merchandizing of the Wombles proved invaluable to them, and they sold over three million badges, in sets of seven.

In 1976 another company made its mark in the character merchandizing field. The newly formed Baynham Presswork got copyrights for the Mr Men, and the sale of these badges did much to set them up as the Wombles had helped the London Emblem Company. The late 1970s saw the market flooded with sets of badges, not only by Rainbow Designs and Baynham and Stanfield, but by other manufacturers. Even Snoopy made his way across the sea from the United States. The early copyright dates on the Snoopy badges are a further indication of how, in the United States, character merchandizing had been around in a big way since Mickey Mouse.

Several bootleg sets also made their way into some of the retail outlets between 1977 and 1980. Bootleg badges do not bear a necessary copyright, which, in 1985, could cost £1,000. Royalties of six to eight per cent were also payable. One of these sets featuring Winnie the Pooh sold particularly well. Another firm produced jigsaw badges. These badges featured characters printed on wooden, jigsaw-like pieces. None of these were legal. By 1980 the market had settled down, and in 1985, 10 years after the Wombles, Rainbow Designs were marketing Beatrix Potter characters, Noddy, Winnie the Pooh, and those flower fairies.

Character merchandizing: Rainbow Designs

All of these examples are from sets by Rainbow Designs (London Emblem Company).
1 Disney set, early 1970s
2 One of a Robin Hood set from the Disney film, early 1970s
3 One of a Wombles set of seven, 1975
4 One of the Flower Fairies set, 1974 onwards
5 Barbapapa
6 One of a Rupert Bear set, 1975
7 Supergirl, part of set, 1975
8 One of Paddington Bear set, 1976 onwards
9 Warner Brothers characters, 1975
10 One of the Winnie the Pooh set from the Disney film, 1976
11 One from the Basil Brush set of four, 1977
12 One from the The Flumps set of six, 1977
13 One from the alphabet and numbers sets, around 1980
14 One from the Thomas the Tank Engine set of eight, 1978
15 One from a Marvel Comics set of 16, 1978
16 One from a Disney characters set, 1979
17 One from a Beans set, 1980
18 Another Disney character
19 One from The A Team set, 1983
20 A magnet back from the Noddy set, 1984

1

2

ORINOCO
3

4

BARBAPAPA
5

RUPERT AND EDWARD
6

SUPERGIRL
7

Please look after this bear
thank you.
8

DAFFY DUCK
9

Tigger
10

BASIL BRUSH
11

POSEY
12

13

14

15

16

BEAN BOPPING
17

18

19

20

Character merchandizing: Baynham and Stanfield

These examples are all from sets produced by Baynham and Stanfield, except one (*3*), made by the Button Badge Company. *2, 4* to *14* and *16* are all inner ring clip designs used by Baynham and Stanfield from 1976 to around 1981–2.

1 One of 26 Mr Men 1½ in (38 mm) designs, 1976

2 One of many 2⅛ in (55 mm) designs

3 One of the Muppet set of 1976–7. Kermit also bears the copyright date 1956 from his early days in the United States

4 A 1977 set of at least 16 Fonz designs from the TV programme *Happy Days*

5 and **6** Examples from two Noddy sets from around 1978

7 One of a 1978 set of Asterix characters

8 One of a 1977 set from the film *Star Wars*

9 One of a 1977 skateboarding set distributed by Taylorscope

10 Also distributed by Taylorscope, a set featuring the TV detectives Starsky and Hutch, around 1978

11 One of at least six Famous Five designs of 1977

12 A 1979 set featuring Worzel Gummidge, Jon Pertwee and Una Stubbs, produced for C G Toys in Exeter

13 One of a 1978 set for the film *Superman*, produced for Factors Etc Company. A similar set was issued in 1978 by Baynham and Stanfield for the film *Grease*

14 One of the 1978 set of at least six Woofits

15 A 1983 design believed from a Tom and Jerry set

16 From a 1979 glitter set published by Glidrose

MR NOISY

1

MR. TALL

2

KERMIT the FROG

3

HEY! HEY!

FONZ IS COOL

4

HALLO·HALLO·HALLO!

5

6

ASTERIX

7

STAR·WARS

8

FRONT UP AND ENDO!

9

DOUBLE

TROUBLE

10

THE FAMOUS FIVE

11

WORZEL GUMMIDGE

12

13

Woofit

14

15

MOONRAKER

JAWS

16

Character merchandizing: 1970 to 1985

1 to **5** Sets by Dodo Designs. *1* is from the Magic Roundabout set produced in 1 in (25 mm) and 1¾ in (45 mm) sizes in 1972 and 1975, and in at least five different designs. *2* is from the Larry the Lamb set of at least four designs, early 1970s. *3* is from the Camberwick Green set of at least four designs, 1972. *4* is from the Hanna Barbera (Dick Dastardly) set of at least four designs, early 1970s. *5* is from the Tom and Jerry set of at least four designs, 1975

6 One of a set of Warner Brothers lithographs supplied by Anabas of Romford in 1973

7 Love is. . . set of 1½ in (38 mm) and 2⅛ in (55 mm) lithographs, copyright Los Angeles Times, 1973, and sold in many colours and designs

8 Diddyman design, early 1970s

9 From a plastic Sooty set, early 1970s

10 A wooden jigsaw badge, one of many bootlegs produced in the early 1970s

11 One of well over 20 Snoopy designs made in the United States and sold in Britain in the late 1970s

12 A bootleg Snoopy design, 1977

13 to **15** *Yellow Submarine* badges, including those 'Blue Meanies' by Tantra Designs, mid-1970s

16 to **18** More Tantra designs, featuring Winnie the Pooh, one of a set, Billy Bunter, and Popeye

19 Sooty, from a late 1970s set

20 One of many Star Wars designs of 1977, issued along with a set by Factors Etc Company

21 From a 1978 Buzby set of at least twelve designs

22 From a Smurf set of 1980 made in the United States and distributed in Britain

23 From a mid-1970s Disney set

24 A moulded plastic Superman, 1980

Foreign badges

North America

Badges of all types have been made in many countries around the world. The biggest industry is in the United States where, in 1896, the button badge business began. Initially sets of badges were given away with cigarettes as well as for presidential campaigns. These badges were celluloid covered, but by 1920 mass-produced lithographed badges became much more common. From 1920 to 1960 the great majority of the American badges were of the lithographed type, the biggest manufacturer being the Green Duck Company of Chicago. The badge boom of the 1960s encouraged the greater use of acetate-covered designs, partly because lithographs could only be produced economically in lots of over 10,000.

From the earliest days the United States produced far greater quantities of badges than anywhere else. Since 1960 American badges became progressively bigger, even enormous 9 in (228 cm) frying pans have been worn. The American industry has also produced more oval-shaped badges, as well as novelties such as the badges that play tunes or sport flashing lights. Compared to British badges, American ones are expensive. A tune-playing badge in 1985 could cost over five dollars, and even a standard button badge cost more than a dollar.

Plastic badges, too, have been highly developed in the United States. A set of injection-moulded, foil-tipped badges in the shape of one of the States, with a pin stud fastening, has proved very popular with locals and tourists alike.

Political badges, especially electoral badges, have been produced in far greater numbers than in Britain. In the jamboree that is an American election campaign, it has become a tradition to wear a badge. Accordingly, such badges are highly collectable. In the United States, badge collecting generally is also far more popular as a hobby than in Britain. This group of badges is one of the most sought-after in the world, and prices seem ridiculous. The 1920 James Cox and Franklin Roosevelt campaign badges are the rarest of all, and some are valued in thousands of dollars. The great value of these button badges caused a flood of imitations to hit America in the early 1970s. As a result, The Hobby Protection Act of 29 November 1973 was passed to try to prevent collectors being cheated. The act forced manufacturers to put the date on any imitations.

Some of the most beautiful American badges are those produced by Whitehead and Hoag at the turn of the century, using a wide variety of colours. It was Whitehead and Hoag who first exported button badges to Europe. In 1985 thousands of button badges were still being exported.

Canada, too, has a highly developed button badge industry. Many famous designs hail from North America. One example is the 'I love New York' design which has appeared in many different forms around the world.

North American badges

This selection illustrates the range of badges produced in North America.
1 One of a set of flags issued with cigarettes at the turn of the century, made by Whitehead and Hoag
2 From the 1920s to the 1960s most American button badges were lithographs, as is this 1941 example by Bastian Bros of Rochester, New York
3 American Union badge, made by Bastian Bros
4 Geraghty and Company of Chicago made this tiny Red Cross lithograph
5 This Beatles lithograph was made by the Green Duck Company for 'Seltoe 6' in 1964
6 and **7** Tourists could collect a set of these moulded plastic state designs in the early 1980s
8 and **10** Monogram Products of Largo in Florida made these moulded plastic designs for Disney around 1982
9 Oval button badges have proved to be more popular in the United States than in Britain
11 Many clubs exist for badge collectors in the United States, especially for those who collect political or cause badges
12 1976 Bicentennial enamel
13 The 'I love New York' design has influenced many badges worldwide
14 An example of a 1984 Los Angeles Olympics design
15 Tourists could watch the stuntmen at Universal Studios in 1979, and buy these 3 in (77 mm) frying pans
16 Santa badges originated in the United States
17 to **20** Canadian badges, including a 1984 Papal visit design

Western Europe

In Europe badges have been slower to catch on than in Britain or America. Sew-on embroidered badges have proved more popular in Europe than the pin-on variety, certainly for the tourist trade. During the badge boom of the 1960s many European countries relied heavily on imports from Britain.

In Holland in the mid-1960s badges were issued in sets with butter. The sets included 'The five continents' and 'Playing cards' and were an unusually small $\frac{3}{4}$ in (19 mm) in size which meant they had to have a stick pin. These badges were nearly all made up in Britain by B Sanders and Sons of Bromsgrove. About the same time badges were being given away or sold in French fairgrounds. Many of these were of the 'philosophical' nature and nearly all were of British manufacture.

When the hippy movement swept through Europe, peace badges were popular, especially in Scandinavia. Although many of these were British made, some were made in Europe. Sweden, in particular, started producing button badges. However, when Norway had a referendum on the Common Market, it was a British firm that supplied 100,000 YA badges and 100,000 NA badges. In Germany too, political badges became popular and they started to produce them locally. The 1985 Greek elections saw button badges in use, some made in America some in Greece. One-inch (25 mm) stick-pin lithographs were also on sale, probably imported from the Far East.

Eastern Europe

In Russia and Eastern Europe the majority of designs are sober place, commemorative or party badges. Badge collecting in Russia is very popular and millions of badges are made. The vast majority of these are stamped aluminium badges which have been paint filled, although in appearance they look like enamels. Popular themes are Russian towns, football teams, sport in general, and Lenin. For the 1980 Moscow Olympics collectors were able to add hundreds of new Russian badges to their collections.

Africa

Many African countries rely on British imports for their badges. In 1980 50,000 button badges with the head of Joshua Nkomo and the message 'Father Zimbabwe' were exported. Millions of badges are exported to Africa by British firms.

The Far East

Lithographs are produced by the million in Hong Kong and exported far and wide. Second-surface printed insert badges and paint-filled stamped metal badges have been made in increasing numbers in the Far East since the mid-1970s. Many of these badges have been imported by America.

In China, The Peking Red Flag Factory produced millions of plastic and metal badges featuring Mao Tse Tung. With the failure of the Cultural Revolution, Peking authorities tried to recover the badges and destroy them. The lowest level of administration in China, the Neighbourhood Committees, were ordered to pay up to one dollar apiece for any badge in an effort to recall and destroy as many as possible.

Foreign badges

Foreign badges rely heavily on American and British designs – and manufacturers.
1 Plastic Norwegian May Day design
2 German solidarity design featuring Ho Chi Minh
3 1974 German plastic design for the Photo Exhibition of Socialist News Agency, 'Socialists all'
4 Plastic Norwegian Social Democrat design
5 to 9 Russian stamped aluminium paint-filled badges. 5 is Lenin. 6 is 1980 Moscow Olympics football design. 7 is the 1980 Olympic mascot, Misha the bear. 8 is the Kremlin. 9 is a Dynomo Kiev soccer badge
10 Stamped, paint-filled Yugoslavian lapel pin badge for Dubrovnik, made by Ando of Zagreb
11 Swedish Per Edberg design, made up by B Sanders and Sons, 'Healthier Norrbotten (area of North Sweden) without alcohol'
12 'The children of our future', a Swedish design
13 A Danish design 'Financial first aid', made up by B Sanders and Sons
14 A French design, from the early 1970s
15 French philosophical lithograph of the early 1970s. One of a set of at least 20
16 Button badge of a Greek political party for the 1985 election
17 and 18 Stick-pin lithographs from Greece, 1980
19 to 21 Red Cross appeals. 19 is from the Second World War Russian Relief Fund which was also active in Britain
22 A second-surface printed badge of the British pop group Culture Club, made in the Far East and sold in the United States
23 Thomas Fattorini Ltd plastic official's badge for the West Africa Games
24 and 26 African button badges exported from Britain. 25 is by Thomas Fattorini Ltd
25 A Japanese button badge (lithograph)

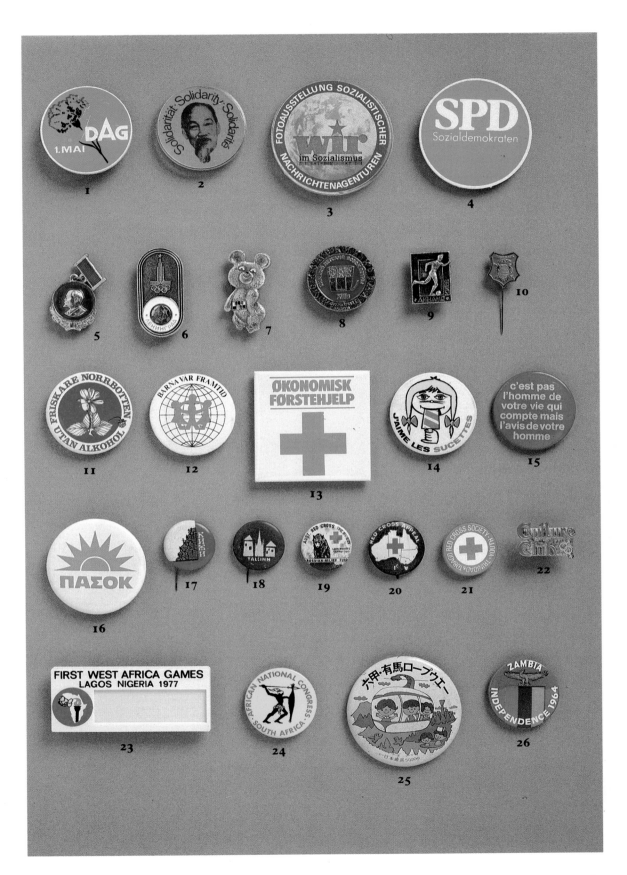

Collecting badges

Becoming a collector

'Goodbye and keep taking the badges' a friend once said to me. Badge collecting, like all good hobbies, can become addictive. Many collectors started when they were children. Some begin by pinning a badge to a hat or jacket and it just builds up from there. Once people know that you collect badges you are on your way to acquiring more and more. Button badges, especially, are throwaway items, and a good collector will get people to throw them his or her way—I have even seen dustmen or roadsweepers with a hatful of badges.

Collectors who start with a few treasured badges find that before they know it they have a tin full, then a box full, and then even more. A very rough estimate is that from 1977 to 1985 one billion button badges were produced for the home market. Seventy-five per cent of these have probably been thrown away, but that still leaves a lot of badges.

When your collection runs into the thousands problems of storage and organization occur. At this point many collectors decide to specialize. Many opt to ignore button badges and go into enamels.

Enamel collectors often begin as specialists anyway, whether it be transport, Butlin's, gollies, trade unions, or football. Enamels are not throwaway items, although plenty are disposed of either accidentally or by neglect. They are generally more valuable than buttons.

Two clubs already exist for enamel specialists. The Association of Football Badge Collectors and the Trade Union Badge Collectors Society. Other collectors are catered for by the Badge Collectors Circle (BCC). In December 1979, a badge exhibition 'Pinned Down' at the Midland Group Arts Centre in Nottingham brought many collectors together for the first time. The interest stimulated by this excellent exhibition resulted in much correspondence among collectors, and resulted in the formation of BCC in 1980. The BCC takes on the mighty task of cataloguing. Specialist representatives for certain categories of badge supply the bi-monthly newsletter with information. As well as an information service, the BCC provides ample opportunity for members to swap and sell.

Obtaining badges

In the late 1970s a special shop opened in London. This, naturally called the Badge Shop, was responsible for a large exhibition, 'Stand up and be Read', in 1980.

As well as obtaining badges through retail outlets, such as bookshops (religious and political ones are especially good), junk shops, gift shops, craft shops, and fashionable shops, flea markets provide the collector with the opportunity of acquiring older badges. Antiques fairs, flea markets, car boot sales, or even jumble sales, may also be sources of old badges.

Prices for Butlin's badges and gollies are rising steadily. These two areas of collecting are extremely popular, and prewar brooches in good condition were fetching over £15 in 1984. Postwar examples fluctuated enormously between £1 and £5. Most enamel badges are generally 50p or more, and many are a lot more. The prices of button badges, on the other hand, vary widely. For modern button badges, 5p to 20p is the normal range. Older designs can be anything from 10p to £5, depending on who is selling and what they think they can get. Royal badges provide some amusement at flea markets. I have purchased a 1953 coronation badge in good condition for 10p and then three stalls away seen a common standard 1977 Silver Jubilee design priced at £1.50.

All button badge collectors should be very careful to get badges in good condition. Slight touches of rust can soon become big patches and the badge is then worthless. Rust spots, especially under the acetate, often spread and this 'foxing', as it is called, leaves you with a sad reminder not to buy a badge in poor condition again.

Many dealers often have little idea of the value of a badge and can be knocked down to a sensible price. Other dealers are more informed, to the extent that popular designs, especially gollies, have been copied. Manufacturers such as R E V Gomm have reissued old designs, and these reissues are stamped R or F, standing for reissue or facsimile.

The practice of copying badges, which could spread to older button badges, is a worry. In the early 1970s it became a huge problem in the United States where a law was passed to prevent it happening.

Advertising for badges locally can be worthwhile; appearing in the press or other media is even better. A lot of collectors, especially children, have featured either on the children's page of their local paper, or on local radio or even television. Such publicity can only help the collection along. Some collectors have had their badges exhibited in local shop windows. Badges can also be seen in museums such as the British Museum, the Museum of London, and the National Railway Museum, as well as many local museums.

Badges acquired directly from retail outlets can be good value. The museum or zoo gift shops don't usually overprice their badges, while some more fashionable gift shops often do, especially if they feature the current craze. If you can resist, it pays to wait until the price comes down. In 1977 skateboarding designs were very popular, and often sold for 25p to 40p. By 1979 they were 10p each in one shop.

One of the joys of button badge collecting is that it is cheap, or it should be. Badges do not cost much to produce, but because so many are lost or thrown away, old examples are often worth a good deal.

Care and display

Looking after your collection is very important. For enamel badges, an occasional clean, and careful handling to avoid enamel chipping off or scratching, is all that is required.

Button badges present a much bigger problem. The two biggest troubles are rusting and fading. Once rust spots get under the acetate the badge is usually ruined. A dry storage place is essential to avoid any moisture destroying your badges. Fading, too, can be a problem. Direct sunlight should be avoided. It is not always a good idea to pin all of your badges up in your bedroom if the sun or moisture can get at them. And if you wear your badges on your hat or jacket fully exposed to the elements you are bound to end up with a rusty set.

Badges you intend to swap can be worn happily and may provide the opportunity for an exchange on the spot. If you do swap a badge it is important to collect information about it. It can take much research to establish the meaning of some badges.

Storage is a big problem if you have a large collection. Some collectors use tins and cigar boxes; others acquire plastic wallets designed for coin collectors. Alternatively, you could cut holes in cardboard and back it with thin stiff card. A pile of these can then be stored in LP cases. This system enables you to arrange the badges exactly as you want, although it is time-consuming to set up. Silica gel or a similar moisture remover can be put into the case to take care of any dampness. Rustproof paper is favoured by some collectors to perform a similar job.

Enamels are harder to store in this way, but as collections are generally smaller, and problems of moisture and sunlight are not so bad, many collectors opt to pin them up. Hessian-covered boards, picture frames, glass cases, offcuts of carpet, and polystyrene have all been used to store and display badges.

As the hobby is growing so fast, and so many youngsters are collecting seriously, future developments will undoubtedly include commercial storage systems. Products to cater for collectors' needs usually develop alongside the hobby; until that time comes for badge collectors, they will have to devise their own systems.

Care of badges

Any collection deserves careful storage and maintenance.
1 and **2** Lithographs are prone to scratching and need careful handling and storing
3, **6**, **7**, **8**, **23**, **24**, **25** The biggest problem for button badge collectors is avoiding rust. Rust spots will spread (*24*), and ruin your badge. Even small rust spots or 'foxing' around the rim will spread (*25*). Bonded acetate is not immune and rust will get in eventually
4 and **5** 'Splitting' of the acetate from the rim is also a problem, and it may lead to ripping (*5*)
9 to **11** Fading is another problem with button badges. *9* is battered as well as faded. *10* is in perfect condition but *11* is the same design after six months of direct sunlight in a shop window
12 to **17** Battered and damaged metal and enamel designs. Enamel will chip if dropped or hit. *12* is the Meccano Guild. *13* was made by Fattorini and Sons, Bradford. *16* A J R Gaunt golly that was not finished properly. *17* National Cyclists Union made by H W Miller
18 and **19** The paint may well rub off paint-filled plastic badges
20 Brittle plastic badge that has snapped
21 and **22** Sometimes button badges are printed off-centre or with errors